THE
COSMIC
ENERGIZER

THE
COSMIC
ENERGIZER

The Miracle Power of the Universe

JOSEPH MURPHY
D.D., D.R.S., Ph.D., LL.D.

Fellow of the Andhra Research University, India

A TarcherPerigee Book

tarcherperigee

An imprint of Penguin Random House LLC
375 Hudson Street
New York, New York 10014

Library of Congress Cataloging-in-Publication Data

Name: Murphy, Joseph, 1898–1981, author.
Originally published: West Nyack, N.Y. : Parker Pub. Co., 1974.
Title: The cosmic energizer : the miracle power of the universe / Joseph Murphy,
D.D., D.R.S., Ph.D., LL.D., Fellow of the Andhra Research University, India.
Description: New York : TarcherPerigee, 2017.
Identifiers: LCCN 2016040846 | ISBN 9780143129851 (paperback)
Subjects: Success. | Occultism.
Classification: LCC BJ1611.2 .M792 2017 | DDC 131—dc23

146119709

PUTTING THE COSMIC ENERGIZER TO WORK FOR A MIRACULOUS NEW LIFE

THERE IS A mystical power within you, which I call the Cosmic Energizer, that can completely transform your life spiritually, mentally, financially and socially and set you on the high road to happiness, freedom and peace of mind. This power lies dormant within you, and when you learn about it and begin to use this mystical power, you can solve your problems, find your true place in life and begin to live the life more abundant.

I have seen men and women lifted up from the midst of frustration, sickness, poverty and despair through the application of the Cosmic Energizer within themselves and made sound, well, prosperous, and full of vitality, energy and enthusiasm. They entered into a life of almost boundless power.

You are connected with this Infinite Power, which can teach you all things. All that is necessary is that you have an open and receptive mind. I have known businessmen, housewives, taxi drivers, short order cooks, men and women from all walks of life, to be inspired into new thoughts and ideas which made them large fortunes, resulting in promotion and far greater opportunities to release their hidden talents.

As you read the various chapters in this book and apply the simple techniques outlined herein, you will attract the right friends, the right partner in life, the ideal associates in your business or professional field, and kindred spirits who harmonize with you and who are interested in the same ideas, plans and purposes. This Cosmic Energizer can furnish you with all the wealth you need, provide you with the ideal house, and the prosperity enabling you to be, to do, to have and to go wherever you want according to your heart's desire.

This Cosmic Energizer is already well known to millions of people throughout the world and has been known to certain illumined people for thousands of years. This Power is the presence of God in man. To be aware of this Power and to utilize It in your life is your divine birthright. In this book you will learn to let this Divine Power flow through your mind, body, business and all other phases of your life so that you need no longer live a life of limitation, lack and difficulties, but will rise up like an eagle with the wings of thought, feeling, imagination and faith to the realm of unlimited resources, dominion and joy.

As you read this book you will realize more and more that this mystic, wonder-working Power is within your own mind, and you can begin to use it immediately, as it is responsive to your thought. This Power is stronger than a laser beam, hydrogen, atomic or nuclear missiles, and more potent than all the energies and explosives in the whole world. It is the Power of the Infinite, or God, unlimited and inexhaustible. When you have read a few chapters of this book you will recognize how men and women have made conscious contact with this Power and set it operating in their businesses, home lives, and financial affairs. All the wonderful results they achieved can be yours also.

I urge you to study this book and to apply the methods of scientific prayer elaborated on herein. As you do, I feel absolutely convinced that you will make use of this miracle-working Power that will banish confusion, misery, lack, melancholy, and failure; it will sever you from emotional and physical bondage and place you on the royal road to the fulfillment of your fondest dreams. The instructions given are in ordinary, everyday language, the same as you find in your daily papers, periodicals and current magazines. The unique feature of this book is its down-to-earth practicality. Here you are presented with simple mental and spiritual formulas which you can apply in your workaday world.

Over 30 years ago, the author of this book decreed silently prior to sleep at night that all his writings would be published in all modern languages. I didn't lift a finger in trying to have it done. The wisdom of my subconscious responded and caused publishers in many countries to seek permission to translate my writings into their respective languages. Today many of my books are translated into French, German, Italian, Portuguese, Japanese and Spanish. This is what happens when you know how to turn over your request to your subconscious mind—results follow in Divine order.

About 24 years ago I turned over a request to my deeper mind as follows: "Infinite Intelligence opens up the way for me to lecture all over the world in Divine law and order." Some weeks passed by and invitations came in from India, Australia,

New Zealand, South Africa, Canada, France, England and Japan. I visited all these countries, lectured there, and got an enthusiastic reception, making lifelong friends. I have revisited many of these countries since then and have conducted classes on mental and spiritual laws. I have appeared on radio and television, both here and abroad. You can use this Power wisely. It is no respecter of persons and will respond to you when you follow the procedures outlined in this book.

The preceding is mentioned solely for the purpose of demonstrating how the wisdom of the Cosmic Energizer responds according to the nature of your request. As a general rule, I avoid making references to myself, but I believe these paragraphs will be of interest to many readers seeking a simple way to get answers from the Infinite Power within us all.

In Chapter 2 you will read about a man born and reared in the ghetto with its attendant limitations. He heard a teacher explain how he could get all the money he needed, and he began to play a game in his mind imagining all the constructive ways he would utilize the money, as if he already had it. From time to time he conducted inner conversations with himself on the wise use of the money. He carried a picture in his mind of graduating from college, opening his own business, traveling all over the world, sending worthy young people to college and paying their expenses. He won a scholarship, married a wealthy woman, graduated cum laude, opened his own business, and prospered in a magnificent way. He eventually retired as a multimillionaire.

Likewise, you can discover in this book why money is simply a thought-image in your mind, and your inner speech can manifest all you want.

In Chapter 1 you will read how a junior executive began to tap the wisdom of the Cosmic Energizer within him and advanced from $40,000 to $200,000 a year. He established a mental pattern in his mind and claimed definitely that the energy of the Infinite passing through the pattern in his mind would cause it to be engraved in his deeper mind. He made a habit of this, and one day while working at the bank he was approached by a man who had conducted large transactions there. This man asked him to head his concern in Texas as financial advisor at a salary of $200,000. Read the complete episode about this man and you, too, will begin to discover the wonder-working power within yourself.

The Cosmic Energizer is instantly available to you, and the only difference between one man rolling in wealth and another who can't make ends meet is that the wealthy man has tuned in to the Cosmic Energizer, either consciously or unconsciously, and it responds to him in avalanches of abundance.

In Chapter 6 you will read a fascinating account of a mother who learned how to apply the healing power of the Cosmic Energizer. Her boy suffered from severe asthmatic attacks which did not always respond to medication. Three or four times a day in her imagination she pictured her boy in front of her, saying, "Mom, God healed me. I feel wonderful." She persisted in this mental image, and at the end of a month the boy was completely free from the paroxysmal attacks of asthma.

There is only one healing power, and this woman knew that her mental imagery and feeling would resurrect the healing power in her son. In other words, she was in rapport with the subconscious of her son, and she impregnated her subconscious and his subconscious also with the idea of wholeness.

In Chapter 7 you will learn how a detective leads a charmed life even though he was shot at 20 times. He knows the Cosmic Energizer responds when he calls upon it. His prayer morning and night is: "The whole armor of God surrounds me. I bear a charmed life. God is my hiding place, and He encompasses me with songs of deliverance." By repetition he has engraved the preceding prayer in his subconscious mind, which renders him impervious to all harm.

By applying this technique mentioned in Chapter 7, you can also lead a charmed life wherever you go, whether by boat, airplane, bus or automobile. Whatever means of conveyance you use, you will be watched over by this overshadowing Presence and be encompassed with songs of deliverance. This book gives you the secret to a charmed life. It is written clearly and distinctly, based on universal laws of mind which never fail. Thousands of people use this great protective prayer and lead charmed lives.

In Chapter 10 you will read how Kenneth Pennington offers a ritual and self-composed prayer-song, and his subconscious responds with an overwhelming urge to dig in a particular area. He finds ornaments, shells, bones, tools, and weapons dating back to primitive times. Museums display thousands of his discoveries. Kenneth is aware of the tremendous powers within him and believes he will be divinely led to the riches he is looking for in the soil.

You can bring into your life more power, more wealth, more health and more happiness by learning to contact and release the hidden power of the Cosmic Energizer. How to bring all these blessings into your life and those of your family is elaborated on in every chapter of this book.

In Chapter 14 you will read how Henry Flagler, the Standard Oil multimillionaire, as reported in *Everybody's Magazine*, stated that the secret of his marvelous success was to imagine a thing as a finished form. He visioned the whole project as completed. Knowing there was oil in the ground, he would imagine tracks on the ground, trains running and steaming, the men going to work talking and laughing, and the train whistles blowing. Flagler was a man starting from scratch. Regularly and persistently he imagined the end, the final result, and all the forces of the Cosmic Energizer came to his aid. He attracted the necessary money, the right geologists, equipment, associates, and all things necessary for the fulfillment of his dream.

Have a goal in life. Focus your attention on it. Imagine the happy ending. Remain faithful to your mental picture and wonders will happen in your life.

The late Dr. Fenwicke Holmes told me that his friend, Arthur Stillwell, built more miles of railroad than any other man of his time and that all his accomplishments were the result of mental pictures which welled up from his deeper mind. The ancients said that imagination was the workshop of God.

In Chapter 17 you will learn about a man who won $150,000 in Las Vegas at one of the gaming tables. He passed on that night and his wife looked everywhere for the money and could not find it. At my suggestion, she quieted her mind and asked that Infinite Intelligence reveal to her the answer.

In the silence she heard what she claimed was her husband's voice telling her exactly where to find the money. It was exact in every detail.

There is that within you that knows all and sees all, and the Cosmic Energizer knows the answer to all questions as it is omniscient, omnipotent, omnipresent and omniaction.

Let this book be a guide and a faithful companion at all times. Go over it frequently and you will open the door to the great treasures of harmony, health, peace and abundance. From this page onward, let us go forward in the understanding of true workable knowledge until the day you have been anticipating breaks for you and you discover that all the shadows of fear, lack and limitation have flown away forever. —*I am come that they might have life, and that they might have it more abundantly* (John 10:10).

JOSEPH MURPHY

CONTENTS

THE
COSMIC
ENERGIZER

1

How the Cosmic Energizer Can Create Riches and Abundance for You

THERE IS ONLY One Fundamental Energy in the world, a Cosmic Energizer, and each one of us is a channel through which this Force is seeking a creative outlet. It is necessary that we become clear channels for the flow of this Divine Energy. Each one of us is a focal point of the Divine, somewhat as an electric bulb may be looked upon as a focal point for the flow of electric current.

This Cosmic Energizer flows harmoniously, peacefully, rhythmically and joyously, and when we let this power flow constructively through us, we are acting in harmony with the Cosmic Energizer, and we will manifest harmony, health, peace and all the riches of the Infinite in our lives. Whenever we indulge in remorse, self-condemnation, resentment or any form of negative thinking, the Divine Energy becomes trapped within us and produces all sorts of trouble.

How to Channel the Riches of the Infinite

The following is a wonderful method for the release of the Cosmic Energizer in you: "I forgive myself for harboring any negative thoughts about myself or anybody else, and I resolve not to do so any more. I radiate love and goodwill to all men and women and to all people everywhere. I know when I have forgiven others, because I can think of them or meet them in my mind and there is absolutely no sting there." This attitude makes a clear and open channel for the Divine Energy.

Pray as follows: "I claim that God's love, light, harmony, truth, beauty, abundance and security flow through me freely and joyously, and I know I am now being prospered and blessed beyond my fondest dreams." Repeat this prayer aloud night and morning three times. As your eyes are focused on these truths and your ears hear them, you now have two faculties working for you, and you will find these truths will sink into your subconscious mind. Since the laws of your subconscious are compulsive, you will be impelled and directed to express God's infinite riches in all phases of your life.

His Idea Was Worth a Fortune

Recently while at a social gathering, an engineer working in a research laboratory told me that members of his staff were pondering and puzzling over a certain research problem for the armed forces. He said: "I got very quiet and relaxed, secluding myself in another part of the building, and said to my subconscious mind, 'I am turning over this request to you, and I know you will reveal the answer to the engineering problem. I am going to let it simmer within you, and when you have the answer you will present it to my conscious mind.'"

The next day he received the answer clearly in his conscious mind and the whole problem was quickly unraveled, saving the company considerable money. He received a promotion, a considerable increase in salary and was made a junior partner in the organization. He will share in the very large annual profits.

He Adopted New Ideas Toward Money and Prospered

A teacher who wished to prosper referred to money as "filthy lucre." I explained to him he had to change his attitude toward money, because his silent condemnation of money caused it to fly from him instead of to him. He realized that it would be foolish to pronounce uranium, lead, cobalt, nickel, copper or a dollar bill as evil. A dollar bill is harmless, and the only difference between it and nickel or copper or any other metal is that the atoms and molecules with their electrons and protons are arranged differently than are those which constitute paper.

Here is the practical, down-to-earth technique he employed which multiplied money in his experience: "From now on I look upon money as Divine substance, for everything comes out of the One Spirit (God). I know that matter and spirit (energy) are one. I claim and decree that money is constantly circulating in my life and that there is always a Divine surplus. I use money wisely and constructively. Money flows to me in avalanches of abundance. Money is an idea in the mind of God, and it is good and very good. God pronounced all things He created good and very good."

This teacher affirmed these truths for about five minutes night and morning, and at the end of a month's time, he was promoted with a big increase in salary. He also received a completely unexpected inheritance from an aunt he had never met. He made it a special point to never deny what he was affirming. Let wonders happen in your life by accepting a new attitude towards the riches all around you.

Life Is Energy

God is Life and that is your life now. Life is power and supply. Remember, the Life Principle is the creative source out of which the world and everything in it was made at the beginning of time, and constant creation is going on now.

How He Went from $40,000 a Year to $200,000

A few days ago on my radio program I told how a $40,000-a-year junior executive in one of the local banks wanted to advance, accomplish greater things, and use his extraordinary knowledge of finances in a far more wonderful and expansive way. Accordingly, he said that he established a mental pattern or mold in his mind and claimed definitely and positively that the energy and vitality of the Infinite passing through the mold in his mind would stamp the desired picture in his deeper mind. He made a habit of this, and one day while working at the bank he was approached by a man who had borrowed a large sum from the bank, who asked him to head his concern in Texas as Financial Adviser and Director. He accepted a ten-year contract and now has a fabulous home, all expenses paid when he travels, liveried chauffeurs, and a $200,000 a year salary. The Cosmic Energizer passed through the picture in his mind and brought it to pass in its own way. This banker's favorite Biblical quotation is:— *What things soever ye desire, when ye pray, believe that ye receive them, and ye shall have them.* (Mark 11:24).

How He Discovered the Riches of Life

Recently I conducted a seminar at the Church of Religious Science in Las Vegas, which is in the charge of an old friend of mine, Dr. David Howe. While interviewing a man in the hotel there, he told me that four years previously when he had arrived in Las Vegas he had only $20 to his name. He promptly got a job as a waiter, however, and sometimes even played the role of a busboy.

A customer in the restaurant where he worked, on observing his industrious attitude, gave him a copy of *Your Infinite Power to Be Rich.** He read it avidly and then he wrote down four things he most desired on a sheet of paper. First was "Riches are flowing to me freely and joyously." Second was "Infinite Intelligence guides me to my highest expression."

Your Infinite Power to Be Rich by Dr. Joseph Murphy, Parker Publishing Company, Inc., West Nyack, N.Y., 1966.

Third was "I have a lovely home in beautiful surroundings." Fourth was "I am happily married to a wonderful woman in Divine order."

Having read the above-mentioned book carefully, and knowing what he wanted, he decided to write down clearly his requests. Every night and morning he would go over these requests, repeating them slowly and deliberately, while knowing that he would draw to himself experiences and conditions similar to his thoughts and imagery. He understood that his technique was a means of impregnating his subconscious mind and establishing the conditions of wealth, success, and harmony in his life. After each period he would give thanks to the Infinite Presence within him for God's riches, true place, his lovely home and companion in life. He was establishing possession in his mind of all that he had requested.

Within three months' time he had accomplished everything he had written down because of his repeated affirmations and his belief in the workings of his mind. He realized that what was impressed on his subconscious would be expressed. A few weeks after he started the prayer process, he was promoted to the position of head waiter. A client of the restaurant introduced him to a very wealthy woman, whom he married. She had a lovely home in Las Vegas, in which he now lives. He has his own business that he and his wife own and operate, and he has others working for him. The couple are very happily married. He said, "It was love at first sight." Now he has all the money he needs to do what he wants to do, and when he wants to do it.

The Cosmic Energizer vivifies, animates, and energizes that which you claim to be true. All the power of the Infinite flows through the focal point of your concentrated attention.—*And all things, whatsoever ye shall ask in prayer, believing, ye shall receive* (Matthew 21:22).—*If thou canst believe, all things are possible to him that believeth* (Mark 9:23).

How He Uses the Cosmic Energizer in His Work

Emerson said, "Nothing was ever achieved without enthusiasm." A young college graduate in electronics and engineering told me that he is intensely interested in the field of electronics. His enthusiasm is thoroughly aroused in this area so that he finds tremendous mental energy released, and marvelous new ideas come clearly into his mind. They come, he said, "out of the blue." He has brought about many innovations and improvements in the electronics laboratory where he works and, although a young man of 22, already earns $30,000 a year, all due to his faith in the Cosmic Energizer and his enthusiasm for his chosen work.

The word "enthusiasm" comes from the Greek, and literally means to be possessed by God. It means an absorbing or controlling possession of the mind by any interest or pursuit. His constant prayer is as follows: "The energy of the Infinite Power animates and sustains me, and creative ideas unfold within me revealing to me everything I need to know." He has faith in the response of the Cosmic Energizer and in the attainment of his goal; then follows enthusiasm, which is awakened by his positive faith. There are times when he feels actually "inspired." Gradually a new world of achievement is opening up for him.

This young engineer's favorite Bible verse is:—*If any of you lack wisdom, let him ask of God, that giveth to all men liberally, and upbraideth not; and it shall be given him* (James 1:5).

SON OF FORMER SLAVE NOW MULTIMILLIONAIRE HEAD OF ONE OF BIGGEST BANKS IN WEST

At 32, railroad cook Milton Grant decided he wanted to make it to the top in business. So he started at the bottom—with a second-hand garbage truck and a third-grade education.

By age 40, he'd made his first million dollars—a startling feat for a poor black man born the son of former Virginia slaves. Says the board chairman and chief stockholder of the Family Savings & Loan Association of Los Angeles:

> I always knew there was a better life and that it was up to me to find it. Very early in life, I learned that good hard cash makes a nice soft place on which to fall.

Hard cash, however, was an item that Grant had very little of as a young man. Born in 1891 in Parkersburg, West Virginia, Grant had to quit school to help support his 11 brothers and sisters.

> I shined shoes and did janitor work for a local shoe store. Later, I got a job as a dishwasher so I could learn how to cook.

The clean white uniforms of cooks really intrigued me. When I was 13, I got a job washing dishes for $2.50 a week on the Chicago Rock Island and Pacific Railroad. I finally worked my way up to chief cook, which was the highest railroad job a black man could hold at that time.

With the railroad, Grant had job security and even social status—but since he was still young, he was bursting with ambition:

With my total savings of $150, I headed for California, where I bought a second-hand truck and started a rubbish-collection firm in Pasadena.

At first, I earned only $20 a month—but I made it my business to always be prompt, neat and reliable. And it paid off. In just a few years I was making $6,000 a month.

Grant then bought a hog farm near Los Angeles and fed his stock with some of the garbage he collected. Again, his profits soared—which enabled him to dabble in real estate and eventually buy a small savings and loan business.

Under Grant's leadership, the Family Savings and Loan grew and prospered. Today it's one of the largest on the West Coast.

The poorest man can become a millionaire if he just sets goals for himself and then works to reach them.

Just remember, all progress starts with yourself. If you sincerely believe that, then you can be whatever you want to be.

This is as true in America today as it ever was.

Grant—who lives very modestly with his wife Flora—
added:

> I don't think of myself as a millionaire, although I
> do have several million. To me, a millionaire's a man
> with a big wad of bills, who rides around in a big
> chauffeured limousine and wears fancy clothes. But
> that's not my lifestyle.
>
> I still drive my own car, go to the office every day, and
> have no plans to retire.

Grant, who says he built his fortune "one brick at a time,"
explained to *The National Enquirer*:

> One reason a dollar won't do as much for people
> today is that most people won't do as much now to earn
> a dollar . . . like I did.

The above is taken from *The National Enquirer*, April
1973 issue, page 19. It tells the whole story of success,
wealth, and achievement. This man came to a decision
that there was a better life, and he had a vision of abundance, security, and the good life. Your vision is what
you are looking at, what you are giving attention to,
and where you want to go in life. Like Milton Grant,
you will go where your vision is. Set a goal for yourself,
become enthusiastic, and above all, have goodwill,
which is love. Love is the fulfilling of the law of health,
wealth, success and victory over problems.

How to Energize Your Desire and
Achieve the Riches of Life

As I was writing this chapter, I received a long-distance phone call from New York City. This caller was distressed and emotionally wracked: bills were piling up, income tax was due, her husband was laid off, and her son's tuition for his last semester in college was overdue. Her home had been for sale for 12 months, and many looked at it but never came back.

I suggested that she try prayer, pointing out that there is an internal source of supply and a universal wisdom which could solve all problems. At my request she wrote down the following prayer:

Ask, and it shall be given you; seek, and ye shall find; knock, and it shall be opened unto you (Matthew 7:7). God, the Cosmic Energizer, gives life to my ideals, desires, and plans; I surrender my home to the Infinite Presence, knowing that I will attract the right buyer, who wants it and who will prosper in it. I accept this now. I recognize that God is my instant and everlasting supply, meeting all my needs at every moment of time and point of space. I give thanks for God's riches, forever active, unchanging and eternal. I give thanks for a wonderful new opening for my husband in Divine order.

She began to affirm this prayer three or four times a day, making certain that she subsequently never denied what she affirmed. The Cosmic Energizer began to flow through her thought images, implanting them in her subconscious mind. An attorney living next door to her bought the home for his son who was getting married. He said that he had noticed the sign "For Sale" recently for the first time, even though it had been there for a year. Her husband was called back to work and promoted. A few weeks following this prayer process, her husband's only sister, who was a spinster, passed on bequeathing $250,000 to him, and all her gold was to come to his wife.

All her problems were solved within a month. The energy does not expand in you until it is released. Remember, everything increases and multiplies after its kind. Energy, vitality, love, skill, ability, and riches are but different forms of the One Power. Sow the seeds of riches, success, guidance, and right actions, realizing that no seed magnifies and multiplies unless it is sown in the soil. Your soil is your subconscious mind.

How He Learned to Pay the Price for Abundance

I explained to a salesman who was making only $6,000 a year that he had to plant the seeds of riches before he could reap the harvest of the good things of life. In other words, he had to give before he could get. He could not give the Cosmic Energizer (God) anything, as It was all in all—the only Presence, Power, Cause and Substance of all things; but all he had to do was to recognize the Cosmic Energizer within as the true Source: Give It attention and loyalty, and then pour energy, life, love and attention on that which he wanted. When he had succeeded in establishing the mental equivalent in his mind, the result would follow. The price he had to pay was belief, and according to his belief would it be done unto him in all phases of his life.

I explained to him the meaning of the Biblical truth:— *Except a corn of wheat fall into the ground and die, it abideth alone: but if it die, it bringeth forth much fruit* (John 12:24). He realized he had to deposit the seed of riches in the garden of his mind and pour the energy of faith, confidence and love into the seed, accelerating its growth and manifestation in his life.

HIS MAGIC FORMULA FOR INCREASE

This above-mentioned salesman started a prayer process by claiming regularly and systematically that the infinite intelligence in his subconscious mind was now attracting to him men and women who wanted what he had to offer, which was real estate. He claimed that they had the money to buy and that there was a Divine exchange in which they prospered and he was prospered. He affirmed knowingly that these prospects gave him their attention and were interested; that he would create confidence and desire on their part; and, having mentally possessed the land in their minds, they would possess it objectively. He knew that possession in the mind was nine points of the law. His sales have increased remarkably, and in the first six months of that year, he had been rewarded with an income of $50,000 in commissions.

He has learned that by giving service and making money for his clients, he has planted seeds in his subconscious, which are bringing him a harvest of inner satisfaction and an abundance of God's riches.

—*Delight thyself also in the Lord; and he shall give thee the desires of thine heart* (Psalm 37:4).

HOW HER INNER SPEECH PRODUCED RICHES FOR HER

In interviewing a young woman a few days ago, she told me that several years previously she had been a stenographer in a government office. One morning she heard me say on the radio to watch your inner thoughts and make sure that they conform to your aim in life. In other words, your inner talking or inner speech must agree with your goal or desire in life. She said, "I realized I was denying inwardly what I desired outwardly, and I stopped it. I realized that if promotion, increase in salary and prosperity were to take place in my life, my inner speech must conform with the fulfillment of my desires."

She had been conducting a mental conversation with herself when she was pondering along these lines: "There is no future there. Salary is very small. I'll never get ahead," etc. Consequently, this inner speech was accepted by her subconscious mind and she remained in that restricted and unhappy situation. She reversed the entire procedure, however, and started a wholesome, constructive, inner speech pattern in harmony with her aims and purposes in life. She wrote out a sentence which to her meant the realization of her heart's desires, and she repeated over and over again many times a day and prior to sleep her prayer, as follows: "I have a wonderful income. I am wealthy, happy and free. I have a wonderful, spiritual-minded husband. I am needed and appreciated. I am expressing myself at my highest level."

She repeated this until she began to feel the reality of what she affirmed. Her inner speech was the same as if all these desires were fulfilled. She knew that her inner speech or conversation would always be made manifest. After about a month, she was promoted to another department at a much higher salary, doing what she loved to do, and the supervisor of that department proposed to her. The writer had the joy of conducting the wedding service.

"Does your inner speech agree with your aim?" Ask yourself that question. If you say, "Oh, yes. My inner talking is exactly the same as I would talk aloud were my aims in life fulfilled," you will enter into the joy of the answered prayer . . . *If two* (your inner speech agreeing with your fulfilled desire) *of you shall agree on earth as touching any thing that they shall ask, it shall be done for them of my Father* (Cosmic Energizer) *which is in heaven* (invisible presence and power) (Matthew 18:19).

POINTS TO REMEMBER

1. There need be no energy crisis. All that is necessary is for man to tune in to the great Cosmic Energizer, the source of all power and energy; and when he asks for guidance and inspiration and new creative ideas, he will get a response fulfilling all his needs. New sources and techniques will be revealed to him in Divine order.

2. Every problem has a solution. For every question there is an answer.

3. Man is learning to take energy from the sun. As he turns to the Cosmic Energizer with faith and confidence, the answer will come. Its nature is responsiveness.

4. A banker made a mental pattern of the salary he wanted, knowing that the Cosmic Energizer would flow through the mold he had made in his mind, and it came to pass in Divine order.

5. A waiter in Las Vegas, after reading *Your Infinite Power to Be Rich*, wrote down four things he desired in life. He went over his requests several times a day, claiming that all these were now fulfilled in his experience, and as he continued faithfully and knowingly, he succeeded in impregnating all four in his subconscious mind, and they came to pass.

6. A young electronics engineer is intensely interested and enthusiastic in his work, which causes a tremendous release of creative energy and new ideas from the Cosmic Energizer. From a salary of $12,000 he has advanced to $30,000 in one year.

7. The son of a slave came to a decision that there was a better life for him. He had a vision of abundance and God's riches for himself and his family, knowing that the Almighty Power would back up his vision. He is now a multimillionaire, head of one of the biggest banks in the West. This is what he said: "The poorest man can become a multimillionaire if he just sets goals for himself and then works to reach them. You can be whatever you want to be."

8. When you want to sell a home, do not think of all the reasons why you can't, but realize there is an Infinite Intelligence that will attract to you the right buyer, who will appreciate your home and prosper in it. As you accept this truth, the deeper currents of your mind will

bring it to pass. Instead of thinking of debts, bills, etc., reverse the procedure and claim that God is your instant and everlasting supply, meeting all your needs now. As you do this, the Cosmic Energizer will flow through you, filling up all the empty vessels in your life.

9. You must learn to pay the price for what you want. This means you must establish the mental equivalent in your subconscious mind. The price you pay is belief. You must give before you can get. You must put the seed in the ground to get a harvest. Likewise, you must let the Cosmic Energizer flow through your ideals, hopes and aspirations, vitalizing and energizing them, and then you will feel the joy of the answered prayer.

10. Claim that the Cosmic Energizer within you is now revealing to you better ways in which you can serve. You will then discover wonders happening in your life.

11. When you are seeking promotion, wealth and marriage, make sure your inner speech, i.e., your silent talking to yourself, conforms to your aim or desire in life. In other words, be certain that your inner talking is the same as it would be if your prayers were answered now. Let your inner speech be from the standpoint of fulfilled desire. Remember, it is your inner speech which is always made manifest.

2

How the Cosmic Energizer Can Cause Wealth to Flow Freely in Your Life

WEALTH MAY BE looked upon as possessing all the desired food, clothing, energy, vitality, creative ideas, inspiration, money and all the comforts of life in this three-dimensional plane. By tuning in regularly and systematically with the Cosmic Energizer within, you can draw from that inexhaustible storehouse everything you need at all times everywhere.

THE MASTER KEY TO MONEY CIRCULATING IN HIS LIFE

Recently I talked with a retired executive who told me of his very poor background in the ghetto with all its limitations. At school he heard a teacher say that if you want to have all the money you need, think of what you would do with it, how you would use it; dwell mentally on all the constructive ways you could utilize it. He said that at an early age he would conduct an inner conversation with himself on the wise use of the money, while claiming that he already had it.

He carried a picture in his mind of graduating from

college, opening his own business, marrying a wonderful girl, traveling all over the world, sending worthy children to college and paying all their expenses, and contributing substantially to the college where they planned to go. He was not thinking of "making money"; he was always considering how he could distribute it wisely, judiciously and constructively. He won a scholarship, married a very wealthy woman, graduated cum laude, opened up his own business and prospered in a magnificent way. He eventually retired as a multimillionaire.

His master secret was his inner speech—his silent conversation with himself. When your inner speech agrees with your aim, such as money, you will receive answers and get results. This man knew intuitively that money is simply a thought-image in the mind and that his inner speech would be made manifest.

It Is Your Right to Have All the Money You Need

You are here to lead a full and happy life. You should have all the money you need to do what you want to do when you want to do it. Some people avoid using the word "money" in their conversation; they speak of "supply" and "abundance" and "opulence." Although what they really mean is money, they have old, weird concepts and think it is wrong to desire money. This makes no sense and is very unreasonable. Realize money is good and very good. It is God's way of maintaining the economic health of the nation.

You are here to expand and unfold spiritually, mentally, financially, intellectually and in all other ways. You should surround yourself with beauty, luxury and all the other good things of life. See money in its true significance—as a symbol and medium of exchange. Money means freedom from want. It means beauty, abundance, refinement, luxury and the good life. Money has taken many forms down through the ages, consisting of such objects as salt, cattle, sheep, beads, and trinkets of various kinds. In ancient times man's wealth was often determined by the number of sheep, goats, oxen or other animals he possessed. Whatever form money takes, you will always have plenty by using the law of your mind in the right way.

How He Created a Steady Flow of Money in His Life

Some years ago a young teller in the bank said to me, "How can I make more money? How can I do what I want to do?" I replied by giving him a simple explanation and pointing out to him that his habitual thinking formed definite paths and tracks in his subconscious mind and that he could have all the money he needed if he directed his mind and inner speech correctly.

I stressed the point that his inner speech is the cause of all the outer experiences in his life. I asked him how he would think, speak and act if he already had the money he was seeking. He said that he would buy a beautiful home for his wife, get a Cadillac car, take a trip around the world and take courses in economics at one of the nearby universities.

I suggested that he begin his inner conversation along this line: "I have a beautiful home. It is wonderful. I am on a trip around the world. I have a beautiful new Cadillac. I am studying economics at Rutgers University." This was his regular inner conversation to himself while on the way to work, while in the bank, while shaving, or while in the restaurant. He never denied what he inwardly affirmed.

All these things came to pass. He is now making far more money than the president of the bank, money is circulating freely in his life, and he has accomplished all the things he set out to do. He was sent to a special course in economics at Stonier, Graduate School of Banking, Rutgers University.

The Bible says—*For by thy words thou shalt be justified and by thy words thou shalt be condemned* (Matthew 12:37). This banker's inner speech or conversations were based on the premise that he already had all these things. They were real in the sense that they were a thought-image in his mind, and you must possess anything you want first in your mind, since all transactions take place there.

He kept his eye on his goals and objectives, realizing and knowing that his inner speech or conversation must manifest on the screen of space. You must establish the mental equivalent of everything you want in your life. Think of what you want with interest. Your thought induces emotion, and when repeated becomes impressed in your subconscious and must come to pass. This is the law of your mind.

HOW YOU CAN HAVE MONEY CIRCULATING FREELY IN YOUR LIFE

Take a little phrase easily inscribed in your subconscious mind and say it over and over again in a sort of lullaby. The following is a very simple phrase: "I claim consciously and knowingly that money is circulating freely and joyously in my life and there is always a Divine surplus."

Take five minutes in the morning and five minutes prior to sleep at night to repeat this phrase and you will discover that the idea of wealth will impregnate your subconscious mind and you will possess a money consciousness. Your conscious mind is the pen, and you are writing the idea of wealth in your subconscious. The latter will respond in ways you do not know.

You must be sure that you do not subsequently deny what you affirm by saying something like, "I can't make ends meet"; "I can't pay the rent"; or "I can't afford a new car." Never use the word *can't* under any circumstances, as your subconscious mind takes you literally and blocks the flow of your good. Repeat this phrase as often as you like. Inasmuch as you know what you are doing and why you are doing it, results will follow. You are applying a law of mind, and whatever you impress on the subconscious will be expressed.

WHY SHE GOT NO RESPONSE FROM HER SUBCONSCIOUS MIND

The Cosmic Energizer is available to all. Its nature is to respond according to the nature of your request. Some years ago a surgical nurse said to me that she was praying for "supply," by which she meant "money," but didn't use the word and admitted that she had been in the habit of calling money "filthy lucre." I explained to her that what we condemn takes wings and flies away, and that actually she was condemning what she was praying for, which made no sense.

During the discussion she came to realize that gold, silver, lead, zinc, copper or iron are not evil. We are using a combination of copper and nickel and paper in our money at present; certainly there is nothing evil or filthy about these metals or paper money. The only difference between one metal and another is the number and rate of motion of the electrons revolving around a central nucleus. One metal can be changed into another through a bombardment of the atoms by the powerful cyclotron. Eventually, gold, silver and other metals will be made synthetically in the laboratory. There is nothing evil in electrons, protons, or electromagnetic waves.

HER CHANGED ATTITUDE CHANGED EVERYTHING

This nurse woke up to the fact that everybody wants money, and not just enough to go around. The urges, desires and impulses we have for food, clothing, homes, automobiles, expression and abundance are all God-given, Divine and good based on the Biblical injunction:—*God, who giveth us richly all things to enjoy* (I Timothy 6:17).

Accordingly, she began to affirm strongly and knowingly: "I know and believe that money is good and very good. God pronounced everything good and very good. By day and by night I am advancing, growing and expanding along all lines. I use money wisely, judiciously and constructively. I am Divinely guided and am expressing myself at the highest level. Money is God's idea, and it is always circulating freely in my life. I am economically healthy. I give thanks for God's riches, ever active, ever present, unchanging and eternal."

She reiterated these truths in the morning, afternoon and evening, making sure that she did not engage in any negative statement or thought regarding money. Then, suddenly she decided to take up medicine, was accepted in medical school, and eventually graduated as a medical doctor. She later married a professor of medicine. Money is now circulating profusely in her life and there is always a Divine surplus.

MONEY FLOWED WHEN HE GOT HIS CONSCIOUS AND SUBCONSCIOUS TO AGREE

A businessman said that he had been praying for prosperity, greater income and better sales; in other words, he wanted more money to accomplish what he wanted to do, but he got no results. Actually, he became poorer. Oftentimes the explanation is the cure, however, as it was in this case. He was using affirmations such as, "I am wealthy," "I am prosperous," "Money flows freely to me," "I am successful."

I explained to him that his subconscious accepts the dominant of two ideas, or the dominant mood or feeling. In talking further to him, I learned that when he said, "I am prosperous," etc., his feeling of lack was dominant so that each affirmation he made called forth the mood of the opposite such as lack, limitation, poor sales, etc., and more lack came into his experience.

He realized that the answer was to get his conscious and subconscious to agree; then there would be no contradiction. The subconscious accepts what we really, consciously believe, our convictions and dominant feelings. He engaged the cooperation of his subconscious mind by affirming, "Every day my sales are improving; more customers come in every day, and they are satisfied and blessed. I am making more and more money every day of my life. I am continuously advancing, growing and moving forward financially."

These statements created no conflict in his mind, as there was nothing within him which said his sales and money could not increase. He found this approach to be acceptable and sound psychologically, and it produced the desired results. He remained faithful to his mental and spiritual practice, and within four months found it necessary to hire two extra assistants to handle the excess business. He found money flowing to him in avalanches of abundance.

Open Your Mind and Heart to the Influx of God's Riches

To walk the royal road to riches of all kinds—spiritual, mental, material, and financial—you must never place obstacles and impediments in the pathway of others; neither must you be jealous, envious or resentful of others. Remember, your thoughts are creative and whatever you think about another you are creating in your own life and experience.

I have discovered that many talented men and women are jealous and envious of former college friends or their associates in business who have gone up the ladder of success and who have amassed wealth and excelled them. Thinking negatively of former classmates or associates and condemning their wealth causes the wealth and prosperity these people are praying for to vanish and fly away. They are praying two ways: I have found that they are saying in one breath, "God is prospering me now" and in the next breath, silently or audibly, they are saying, "I resent that fellow's wealth, promotion, or increment," as the case may be.

I have found that when they change their attitude and sincerely rejoice in the success, promotion, wealth and riches of others, they prosper beyond their fondest dreams. This is based on an age-old truth taught by the ancients thousands of years ago: "The ship that comes home to my brother comes home to me."

FROM RAGS TO RICHES

At 13, Peter Traynor earned $4 a day as a farm laborer near Boston while his poor immigrant parents struggled to make a new life in the U.S.

Today at 34, he's a multimillionaire.

"Now I'm earning more like $4 a minute," says Traynor, who heads Leverage Funding Systems, a Los Angeles corporation that invests money exclusively for over 1,500 physicians.

"I learned to think success from my father," explains Traynor. "He sold neckties and second-hand clothing for a living before World War 2. I remember he'd load the clothes into our old clunker of a car and wouldn't come home till he'd sold them all—even if it took until midnight.

"As a Polish immigrant, my dad had very Old World attitudes toward money and hard work."

With success as his constant goal, Traynor has managed to put the Midas touch on almost every job he's held.

"Everything I do is geared toward success," he said. "In high school I mowed lawns each day after classes. That soon led me into a part-time landscaping business, which was earning me $18,000 a year by the time I was a junior."

After putting himself through Boston University, Traynor headed West in 1961.

"I came to California for success," he explained to *The Enquirer.* "I observed successful men and emulated their styles, their techniques and their disciplines."

First, he took a job with the Penn Mutual Insurance Co.—and broke a company record by selling $3 million worth of insurance in his first year. In his third year, Traynor wrote $12 million worth of insurance—establishing himself as the industry's number one super-salesman. Though riding the peak of success, Traynor soon left Penn Mutual in his search for still higher peaks. He decided to form his own investment company.

I got the idea after learning that doctors are the best prospects for buying insurance," said Traynor, who says he's worth about $6 million today.

"I knew doctors had money—but also knew they often didn't have time to wisely invest it themselves."

"So I started Leverage Funding to make their money go to work for them—and for me too."

Traynor admits to owning what is "Very definitely the controlling interest" in the corporation, which he said made profits of over $2 million last year, and he also has controlling interest in Lester-Traynor Productions, Ltd., a firm that is venturing into filmmaking.

"Success is just a matter of applying yourself in the right way. If you analyze things carefully and move logically, there are really very few ideas that are impractical," said Traynor, who lives in a large home in the fashionable Trousdale Estates near Hollywood.

"But you pay a price for success. For me, the highest price is the time I spend away from my wife Marney and our four children."

The above article appeared in the September 2, 1973 issue of *The National Enquirer*, by Lloyd Watson. All Peter Traynor had was a good idea, and as he nourished and sustained it, his subconscious compelled him to attract riches in a magnificent way. You can also think "success," think "wealth," think "riches." Your subconscious will magnify and multiply your good a thousandfold in ways you cannot now imagine.

POINTS TO REMEMBER

1. By tuning in regularly and systematically with the Cosmic Energizer within, you can draw from that inexhaustible storehouse everything you need at all times everywhere.

2. If you want a lot of money, think of what you would do; talk and act as if you had all the money you need to do what you want to do. A man amassed a great fortune by conducting an inner conversation with himself on the wise use of money. His inner speech conformed to his aim in life, and when the two agreed, his prayer was answered. He was constantly thinking how he could

distribute the money wisely, judiciously and constructively. He pictured in his mind all the things he wanted to do, and all of them came to pass. Your inner speech or conversation (your thought and feeling) is always made manifest. *And the Word* (thought-image) *was made flesh* (made manifest) . . . (John 1:14).

3. You are here to lead a full and happy life. You should have all the money you need to do what you want to do and when you want to do it. Realize that money is God's way of maintaining the economic health of the nation. Money, in whatever form it takes, is good and very good. Look upon money as a symbol of freedom, beauty, abundance, refinement, luxury and the good life. Be friendly with money and you will always have all you want.

4. A banker discovered that his inner speech was the cause of all the outer experiences of his life. He began to think, speak and act as if he already had the money he was seeking. In other words, he was thinking from the desired end in the same way as if he actually physically possessed all the things he was seeking. His inner conversation was, "I have a beautiful home now"; "I have a beautiful new Cadillac," etc. He discovered his inner speech—his quiet, inner talking to himself—brought forth all his desires, and money circulates in his life freely and copiously.

5. There is a simple formula that enables you to have a steady flow of money in your life to meet all your requirements. Take a little phrase, easily graven in your subconscious, and repeat it over and over again. It will sink into your subconscious, and since the law of your

subconscious is compulsive, you will be compelled to express wealth. Use this phrase: "Money is circulating freely in my life and there is always a Divine surplus." Do not at the same time or subsequently deny what you affirm.

6. A nurse was habitually referring to money as "filthy lucre" while at the same time she wanted lots of money. She learned that when she condemned money it took wings and flew away. She had been condemning what she was praying for, which is inexcusable and too absurd for words. She intelligently changed her attitude and everything was altered. She began to affirm that she liked money and pronounced it good and very good. Her favorite phrase, which she conveyed to her subconscious, was: "Money is God's idea, and it is always circulating in my life. I am economically healthy." She also prayed for Divine guidance, and everything in her life changed. She achieved a wonderful marriage, graduated as a medical doctor and wealth now flows to her in avalanches of abundance.

7. A man who believed in lack and limitation was affirming, "I am wealthy," "I am prosperous," and was gradually getting poorer. He learned that his conscious and subconscious had to agree in prayer. Accordingly, he began to affirm, "Every day my sales are improving. More customers come to my store. I am making more and more money every day of my life. I am continually advancing, growing and moving forward financially." These statements created no conflict in his mind, and they produced the desired result. Within four months

he had to hire two extra assistants to handle all his customers.

8. A great stumbling block to many people in attaining wealth is that they are jealous and envious of the riches of others, not realizing that whatever you think about the other you are creating in your own mind, body and conditions. Your thought is creative, and to be jealous and envious of others is to actually impoverish yourself and attract more lack and limitation. The thing to do is to rejoice in the success of all those around you and to wish for them health, wealth and all the riches of the Infinite. As you do this sincerely and honestly, you will discover that the ship of riches that came home to your brother will also come home to you. Love (goodwill) is the fulfilling of the law.

9. Peter Traynor, who was a $4 a day laborer, had the idea of "success and riches" uppermost in his mind and went from rags to riches on a magnificent scale. He is worth over $6 million today. He started the Leverage Funding Company and invested money wisely for 1500 doctors. In making money for them, he made it also for himself. You too can have an idea worth a fabulous fortune.

3

How the Cosmic Energizer Can Bring You the Good Things of Life

ABRAHAM LINCOLN SAID: "I have been driven many times to my knees by the overwhelming conviction that I had nowhere else to go. My own wisdom, and that of all about me, seemed insufficient for the day."

Socrates said: "Our prayers should be for blessings in general, for God knows best what is good for us."

Tennyson said: "More things are wrought by prayer than the world dreams of. What are men better than sheep or goats that nourish a blind life within the brain, if knowing God, they lift no hands of prayer both for themselves and those who call them friends?"

Coleridge said: "He prayeth best who loveth best."

Whittier said: "The simple heart that freely asks in love, obtains."

Ralph Waldo Emerson said: "Is not a prayer a study of truth, a sally of the soul into the unfound infinite? —No man prayed heartily without learning something."

Bunyon said: "In prayer it is better to have a heart without words than words without a heart."

There is an old proverb that says: "What men usually ask for, when they pray to God, is that two and two may not make four."

When you pray, do not try to change the Cosmic Energizer, which is God, for God is the same yesterday, today and forever. Effective prayer is aligning yourself with that which is true of God and which becomes a focal point for the expression of life, love, truth, beauty, joy and abundance in your life. In other words, prayer is the contemplation of the truths of God from the highest standpoint.

The Cosmic Energizer does not suspend its laws for anybody; neither does it play any favorites. It is impersonal and no respecter of persons. Prayer is the response of the Cosmic Energizer to your habitual thinking and imaging, as well as to your belief. In a certain sense there are as many forms of prayer as there are people in the world.

He Prayed the Prayer of Petition

Recently I talked to a sailor whose ship had been torpedoed in the last world war. He was adrift for ten or twelve hours on a makeshift raft. He said that he cried aloud: "Oh, God, save me! You know I'm here." To him God was an anthropomorphic being existing up in space somewhere. He did not know the laws of mind: that God was the Spirit within him, omnipresent, without face, form or figure, and instantly available to all men. His begging and beseeching did not reach the

Cosmic Energizer, but his blind belief did. When he was rescued by a Norwegian ship, the captain said that for some reason or another he changed his course and the sailor adrift was espied by a sailor on watch on the ship.

The reason for the man's rescue was that he went all the way out on the limb, trusting implicitly that he would be saved. The Cosmic Energizer responded according to his blind belief.

YOUR THOUGHT IS YOUR PRAYER

To pray means to think from the standpoint of universal principles and eternal verities in the same manner as an engineer thinks from established principles of mathematics or a chemist from the standpoint of the laws underlying chemical combinations. Every thought, in a certain sense, is a prayer for the simple reason that every thought tends toward action and manifestation. The Bible says:—*The word was God* (John 1:1). A word is a thought expressed and you are told it was God, meaning it is creative, for there is only one creative power, i.e., the Cosmic Energizer. Your thought, being creative, is, therefore, God also.

All of us have a common Source and we are made of one universal Substance. The Bible says:—*After this manner therefore pray ye: Our Father* . . . (Matthew 6:9) which means all of us come forth from the one Life Principle, or Cosmic Energizer; therefore, in Truth, we are all related. It is essential, therefore, when you pray to have love and goodwill for all men and women everywhere, as well as for the beasts of the field, and everything else in the world. Man must sense his essential unity with all things: the birds of the air, the fish of the sea, and indeed all growing things.

The Cosmic Energizer creates all things and everything is made inside and out of It. No one thing in the universe can be in opposition to another, for the Cosmic Energizer can't be at war with Itself. We are all parts of one stupendous whole, whose body nature is, and God is the soul.

How to Pray in the Right Way

There are many levels and modes of prayer. The old maxim says, "When your thoughts are God's thoughts (constructive, based on principle), God's power is with your thoughts of good." Prayer is essentially thinking from a constructive standpoint. The right way to pray consists of the spiritual premise that there is a Cosmic Energizer within each of us that becomes the thing we desire, to the point that we accept this as true. Your constructive thought action is in tune with the Cosmic Energizer, and It responds according to the nature of your thought.

True prayer is a sustained, constructive attitude of mind that results in conviction. Once your desire is deposited in your subconscious mind, the answer is made manifest as part of a Creative Law. The acid test of whether or not you have reached a conviction is when your mind accepts the idea completely and you can't conceive of the opposite.

Why Her Prayers Were Not Answered

The tendency of the Life Principle, or Cosmic Energizer, is to heal, restore, prosper and bless humanity in countless ways; otherwise, there would be no design, no chemical affinity, no uniting forces in this universe. There is a built-in principle of wholeness and unity in every organism. In the Book of James it says:—*Ye ask, and receive not, because ye ask amiss* . . . (James 4:3).

Mrs. B. had ulcers and was taking medicine prescribed by her doctors, but was nevertheless constantly saying, "The medicine is no good. My ulcers are worse." All her thoughts were of a bitter ulcerated nature; she was resentful and full of hostility and suppressed rage toward relatives. She was at the same time petitioning a God afar off up in the skies somewhere to heal her condition, which she ignorantly inflicted on herself. She was praying with a mind and heart full of hostility, suppressed rage and resentment, which is praying amiss.

HER REVERSED ATTITUDE TRANSFORMED HER LIFE

Following a simple explanation as to what she was doing to herself, she decided to release her relatives, as follows: "I completely surrender my in-laws to the great ocean of Life, wishing for them harmony, health and peace. Whenever any one of them comes to my mind, I will immediately affirm: 'I released you—God be with you.'"

She also decided to stop criticizing her doctors and the medicine, realizing that when she no longer needed a crutch she would be healed, and in the meantime, she should stop finding fault with herself and others. She also realized that her angry, negative thoughts had produced her ulcers and it stood to reason that harmonious, peaceful, loving thoughts would restore her to wholeness.

The Prayer That Freed Her

She made a habit of affirming the following truths of life: "I am at peace with all men and all things. I am Divinely guided in my eating and drinking. I am filled with the peace, harmony, strength, vitality and energy from the Cosmic Energizer. The Life forces flow freely, joyously and harmoniously through my whole being and I am whole and perfect."

As she continued saturating her mind with these truths, and since she had forgiven herself for entertaining negative thoughts and had released her relatives, a wonderful sense of peace came over her. She has now found a new life and is kinder, nobler and more efficient in every way.

How He Dissolved an Acute Problem

A few months ago, a doctor friend of mine became involved in a serious law suit. He was very much annoyed, perplexed and deeply resentful because of the lies and false accusations hurled at him by his opponents. The law suit was not progressing satisfactorily for him. I explained to him that he would have to eradicate his hostility and resentment first before he could pray successfully.

He began to affirm regularly and systematically: "Infinite justice, love, harmony and truth of the Cosmic Energizer operate in the minds and hearts of all involved in this law suit, and the truth is my shield and buckler." Whenever the thought of his opponents came to his mind, he affirmed: "God's love fills your soul." After about a week or so he had a deep feeling of peace, and when the case reached the Appeals Court, it was dismissed.

LOVE IS THE GREAT MAGNET

This doctor said to me that since he had reversed his attitude, he had discovered that love is like a magnet of iron which draws to itself its own. Likewise, he was attracting more and more patients and had remarkable healings.

HIS WIFE SAYS, "MY HUSBAND IS NOW MAGNETIC"

Magnetism is simply an emanation from the Cosmic Energizer. It is the love, the power and the vitality that he is radiating to all those around him. He has transformed himself and is constantly giving out a current of love, and all who come within his orbit are blessed. Before his transformation, he was angry, hateful and resentful and had no magnetism. He was losing patients and money. He had actually shut off the currents from the Cosmic Energizer. He has discovered however, that Divine love dissolves everything unlike itself.

HOW A MENTAL BLUEPRINT TRANSFORMED HER LIFE

A few months ago I gave a lecture to a small group at a private home in Maui, one of the lovely islands of Hawaii. One of the guests there told all of us how she had transformed her life. She pointed out that she had read many books on prayer therapy, positive thinking and mind training, yet her life was a mess; it was lonely, frustrating, and financially embarrassing, and she had only a part-time position.

Eight words in the Bible, however, changed her life:— *Faith, if it hath not works, is dead* . . . (James 2:17). She dabbled with painting as a hobby and one day she painted the kind of house she wanted, a sort of mental blueprint. She pasted it in a section of a large sheet of paper. On still another section she wrote down "$25,000 a year salary." On another section she pasted, "I am happily married to a wonderful man." Then she painted a picture of a swimming pool with a wire fence around it. She pinned this large sheet of paper up in her apartment where she could look at it frequently. She knew that these pictures would gradually form a mental mold through which the Cosmic Energizer would flow, energizing and vitalizing all her desires.

Gradually she impressed her subconscious mind. Desire coupled with belief were the finishing touches to her mental exercise. She said that after a few weeks she could actually feel herself possessing all these things. Mental possession is nine points of the law and the manifestation follows.

How the Answer Came

Shortly thereafter, during a visit to Honolulu for dental appointments, she met an old friend at the Royal Hawaiian Hotel. He introduced her to his brother, who fell in love with her at first sight and married her. He now gives her an allowance of $25,000 a year to spend as she likes. She has a wonderful home in Sydney, Australia, a swimming pool and a marvelous husband.

All of us were impressed by her simplicity, her faith and confidence in the laws of mind, and the wonders of the Infinite Power within all of us. Her favorite quotation is: "I desire to win and I accept the Power within."

POINTS TO REMEMBER

1. Coleridge said: "He prayeth best who loveth best."
2. When you pray, you do not try to change the Cosmic Energizer, which is the same yesterday, today and forever. Prayer is aligning yourself with the eternal verities of life and becoming a focal point for the expression of life, love, truth, beauty and the life more abundant.
3. The prayer of petition works occasionally; i.e., when a man goes all the way out on a limb and trusts what to him is a God in the skies. The real truth of the matter is that he answers his own prayer. The Cosmic Energizer responds to his blind belief.
4. In a certain sense your thought is your prayer for the simple reason that every thought tends to action and manifestation. There is only one Creative Power, namely the Cosmic Energizer, which permeates all life. Your thought is the only immaterial power you know. You are what you think all day long.
5. When you pray it is essential that you be at peace with all men and all things. Realize your essential unity with all life, for God is Life or Spirit, and one part of Spirit can't be antagonistic to another part of Spirit, as Spirit, or God, is one and indivisible. When you are at peace with the whole world, the Cosmic Energizer flows through you filling up all the empty vessels in your life.
6. When your thoughts are God's thoughts, God's power is with your thoughts of good. Prayer is essentially thinking from a constructive standpoint. True prayer consists of

the spiritual premise that the Cosmic Energizer becomes the thing you desire to the point you accept this as true.

7. The tendency of the Cosmic Energizer is to heal, restore and prosper you.

8. A woman had ulcers due to bitter thoughts of hostility, resentment and rage. She learned that in order to get a healing, she had to cease all criticism and condemnation of others and to forgive herself for harboring negative thoughts. She began to bless all those who irritated her. She made a habit of praying as follows: "I am filled with the peace, harmony, strength and vitality of the Cosmic Energizer, and I am made whole and perfect." She found her health and peace in this changing world.

9. A doctor was involved in a bitter lawsuit. When he decided to eradicate his resentment and hostility, he was able to pray effectively. Whenever the thought of his opponents came to his mind, he affirmed: "God's love fills your soul." He also began to claim boldly that the infinite justice, harmony and truth of God prevailed, and the case was finally dismissed.

10. This doctor discovered that love was a great magnet, and he found that he attracted more patients and had remarkable healings. Love dissolves everything unlike itself.

11. A woman painted the kind of a home she wanted with a swimming pool and pasted it on a section of a large sheet of paper, adding some written requests such as, "I'm married to a wonderful man. I have an income of $25,000 a year." She placed the sheet of paper in a prominent place in her apartment and gazed at it many times

a day, knowing she was impregnating her subconscious mind. The Cosmic Energizer flowed through her mental mold, fulfilling all her requests in Divine order. Her favorite maxim is: "I desire to win and I accept the Power within."

4

How the Cosmic Energizer Can Reveal Answers and Transform Your Life

A FEW YEARS ago while traveling by train from Dublin to Cork, I noticed a man carrying a bag on his back, and the conductor said to him: "You can take that bag off your back. The train can carry both of you." And this reminded me of the fact that there are a great many people carrying the burden of grief, sorrow, grudges, peeves, bitterness and hostility, which robs them of vital energy, creating short-circuits in their lives. Like the leakage of electricity, the Cosmic Energy in their lives is dissipated and wasted.

HOW THE COSMIC ENERGIZER RELIEVED HER OF HER BURDEN

Recently I interviewed a woman who had followed a scientific diet prescribed by her physician and who had taken off 40 pounds for a time, but in the past few months she was, as she said, back where she started, 40 pounds overweight. I explained to her that the basic reason for her overweight was the burden she was carrying in her mind, and when she followed the great truth, *Cast thy burden upon the Lord* (Law), *and he shall sustain thee* . . . (Psalm 55:22), she would be free.

THE CAUSE OF HER OVERWEIGHT

Her burden consisted of a deep hatred for her husband, together with a suppressed rage. She had discovered that he had been unfaithful and had pretended to forgive him. However, by hating him, she was also hating herself, because she was thinking hateful thoughts and generating negative emotions. All hatred is self-hatred, which is a deadly poison. Her self-loathing had caused her to put on aprons of flesh so that she would be repulsive to men. The explanation oftentimes is the cure.

I explained to her that the Cosmic Energizer flows harmoniously, peacefully, joyously and rhythmically, but that this flow of vital energy had been dammed up by her, bringing on her fatigue, exhaustion, insomnia and migraine. I suggested she throw out of her mind everything that was not contributing to her beauty, charm, vitality and peace of mind. She realized what she was doing to herself—actually generating mental poisons which robbed her of peace, health and happiness.

She came to a clear-cut decision and forthwith discontinued living a lie. She directed her attorney to get a divorce for her; she also decided to face her husband and his paramour and tell them that she wished for them all the blessings of life.

How Her Freedom Came

She decided to become a focal point for the Cosmic Energizer and claimed boldly that the vitalizing, energizing power of the Infinite was flowing through her and that Divine love was saturating her whole being. Knowing that as she aligned herself with the Cosmic Energy which is love, love would dissolve everything unlike itself. She discovered after a while that all ill will, bitterness and hatred had melted away.

Every night prior to sleep, she affirmed: "I weigh 120 pounds in Divine order through Divine love." After a few weeks she lost all desire for amylaceous and fatty foods which had contributed to her overweight. She regained her beauty, grace and charm, and she also discovered that—*Love is the fulfilling of the law* (Romans 13:10).

The Cosmic Energizer Seeks to Express Itself as the Life More Abundant

Cosmic Energy moves constructively, harmoniously, rhythmically and joyously. When we go against the principle of harmony and love or think and act in any way contrary to the forward tendency of Life, we suffer; but we have inflicted the punishment upon ourselves.

How to Generate Energy for Your Plan

You can definitely cause the Cosmic Energy to flow when you have a certain plan, aim or goal in life. You go where your vision is. Your vision is what you are looking at in your mind, what you are giving attention to, the ideal you are focused on. When you realize you can reach your goal, the Cosmic Energizer flows on your behalf, attracting to you everything you need for the fulfillment of your dream.

How He Envisioned His Plan

One of the listeners to my radio program in Los Angeles, which is heard throughout most of Southern California, wrote and said: "I learned from listening to your program that I had been blocking my own good because I was constantly blaming the boss, the organization, my wife or somebody else for my unhappy experiences and lack of funds. I decided to lighten the load after I heard you explain the meaning of casting the burden. I now know that my anger was burning up my precious energy at a very rapid rate, and it had affected my glands and my blood pressure and was bringing on complete exhaustion and depletion of my vital energy."

The above is a digest of a long letter, but it shows how criticism, condemnation of others and suppressed rage debilitate the entire organism and goes contrary to the normal flow of the Cosmic Energizer. He learned that it makes no difference how others act or what they do. The thing that matters is how he reacts. Actually, it was the movement of his own thoughts which had caused all his trouble and impeded his progress. It is not what others do; it is our thoughts about it that matters.

How He Cast the Burden, Opening the Way
for the Cosmic Energizer to Flow

He saturated his mind with the following truths, knowing that by repetition, faith and expectancy they would sink into his subconscious mind and come forth into his experience and operate in all phases of his life: "I know that all men are my brothers. All of us have a common Father. I see the Living God in everyone I meet. I salute the Divinity in each person. The Love of God flows through me to all mankind. I bless all those who criticize me. I pray for those who speak ill of me. I rejoice to see others succeed. I loose everyone now and I let them go in peace. I open the windows of my mind; I let in the influx of the Holy Spirit. I am perfect and cleansed. I am at peace. The Love of God fills my mind; all is well. I reflect the Love of God; I am absolutely loving toward all. I am conscious of God everywhere because God is over all, through all. I know that the action of God is taking place in the mind and hearts of all. It is wonderful!"

In a month's time his whole life had been transformed. He no longer burned up the vital energy. He had found peace within, and having found love within, he had found it waiting for him everywhere. He has now also opened the channels for wealth and health.

How She Ceased Wasting Vital Energy

Take us the foxes, the little foxes, that spoil the vines: for our vines have tender grapes (Solomon 2:15).

A government secretary came to have a consultation with me, saying that her problems in the office were due to the "little foxes that spoil the vine." She was highly sensitive and said that other girls who were her fellow employees were jealous and envious of her, and that they carried tales and lies about her to the supervisor. She was resenting the girls and placing herself in a house of bondage and thralldom—all self-imposed. She was giving power to others to hurt her and was burning up vital energy, resulting in nervousness, the all-gone feeling, and complete exhaustion at night, accompanied by insomnia.

At my suggestion she ceased giving attention to the petty annoyance, negativities and gossip of the office. These trivial irritations were consuming so much of her inner energy, they caused her to make mistakes, which in turn kept her mind off that which is lovely and of good report. It was also preventing the flow of all good from the Cosmic Energizer, the Source of all blessings.

How She Got Back on the Beam

Every morning as well as other times during the day, she identified herself with the Cosmic Energizer and affirmed boldly: "God is my boss, my employer, my way-shower, my guide, my counsellor, my source of supply. I give all my allegiance, loyalty and devotion to the Supreme Power within me. God guides me, watches over me, sustains and strengthens me, and I am energized from On High. God thinks, speaks and acts through all the girls in the office, and whenever I think of any one of them, I affirm immediately, 'God loves you and cares for you.'"

She adhered faithfully to these truths and found that as she changed inside, the outward picture changed also. She has found peace in this changing world. She ceased carrying the dead, useless burdens of resentment, anger and hostility. These are the little foxes that spoil the wine of life, which is the exhilarating and vitalizing flow of Cosmic Energy coursing through our entire system. She has gone up the ladder of life and is now a supervisor. Her journey is onward, upward and Godward.

Looking Upon Life as a Current of Energy

Paul says—*Faith which worketh by love* (Galatians 5:6). The love of which Paul speaks is the feeling in your heart of goodwill to all. It is an emanation or outreaching of the heart to all when you rejoice in seeing people as they ought to be: happy, joyous and free. Love frees, gives; it is the Spirit of God in action. Love is also that inner feeling whereby you give all allegiance, loyalty and recognition to the One Power—the Cosmic Energizer—and you pay no attention to any person, circumstance or condition or anything else that would tend to swerve you from your good.

She Looked Upon Life as a Current

A Mrs. B., whose husband had passed on a few years ago, felt lonesome, bitter and hostile. She felt somewhat isolated from her family, who lived in the East and who never wrote her or communicated with her in any way. At my suggestion, she started to cast aside the burdens of self-doubt, loneliness, criticism of relatives, and dislike of others in the retirement center. She began to discard everything that was not contributing handsomely to her welfare. She began to affirm frequently to herself the following:

"The Cosmic Energizer is flowing through me as a current of life, love, truth and beauty, creating pleasant relations, harmony, abundance and security in my life. I am a focal point for the Cosmic Energizer, and my mind and heart are open for all the blessings of life. I give thanks for a wonderful trip to Europe and for God's riches flowing to me from all angles. I live by the law of love, and I wish for everyone what I wish for myself."

She reiterated these truths many times a day, which formed a nucleus around which the Cosmic energy began to flow. A few short weeks went by and then, out of the blue, her daughter, who lived in the East, phoned her asking her to join her on a trip to Europe which extended for six weeks, all expenses paid. On this trip she met a retired professor; they got married in London and have now settled down in Spain to live out their years in happy retirement.

She wrote me recently saying she has never been so happy. She tends the garden, gives English lessons twice a week to sons and daughters of neighbors, and is having the time of her life. She commented that she no longer holds the memory of grudges, peeves and ill will. She also realized that her previous sense of guilt had reduced her to a kind of slavery and that she now realizes she had been constantly trying to compensate for her low opinion of herself.

Learn to Accept Forgiveness

Forgive yourself. Have a high estimate of yourself. You are a son or daughter of the Infinite. Have a healthy, reverent, wholesome respect for the Divinity that created you, watches over you and that created the whole universe and all things therein contained. Make a habit of exalting the Divine Presence within you. One of the quickest ways in the world to eradicate an inferiority or rejection complex is to look in the mirror for about five minutes every morning and evening and affirm out loud, feelingly and knowingly:

"I exalt God in the midst of me, mighty to heal, restore, beautify and magnify my good in countless ways." You will be amazed how you will activate the Cosmic Energizer, which will flow as currents of love, peace, harmony and abundance into your experience.

He Erred in Trying to Compensate for Guilt Feelings

A junior executive in a large organization was continually mentally belittling his associates. He made a sort of fetish of finding fault with all those around him in the office. He was full of criticism about their abilities, talents, morals and ethical standards. I pointed out to him that actually what he was trying to do was to drag them down to his own level, while in the meantime trying to exalt himself; that in reality he was projecting his own shortcomings and sense of inferiority on to them. He did not like what he saw, and this attitude resulted in his hostility and pugnacity. This young man was really wasting his vital energy in this running battle in his mind, causing him to lose his grip on the flow of the life more abundant.

How He Transformed Himself

This man had a submerged sense of guilt going back to an early marriage. During the pregnancy of his wife he had deserted her, divorced her in Mexico and remarried. Apparently they quarreled and were hopelessly incompatible; and because of his sense of guilt, he was always on the defensive, sensitive and highly irritable.

The Explanation Is the Cure

I asked him: "Would you desert your wife now?" He answered, "No. I'm very happy and have two wonderful children." I pointed out to him that he was not the same man who deserted his other wife twenty years previously—emotionally, physically, mentally or spiritually—for the simple reason that he was leading a good life now and sincerely wanted to continue to lead a full and happy life. The Life Principle does not punish; we punish ourselves by misuse of law and by negative thinking. But the minute a man decides to change his thoughts according to the eternal verities, there is an automatic response from the subconscious mind, and the past is forgotten and remembered no more. A new beginning is a new end. Begin to fill your mind with faith, confidence, love and goodwill, and the result will be health, happiness, peace and security.

With the aid of his attorney this man made a sincere effort

to locate his former wife, who had remarried. He found she had a daughter, who was his own. He sent an anonymous gift of $30,000 to her on the advice of his lawyer. This gave him a marvelous sense of relief. He began to exalt God in the midst of himself and also practiced radiating love, peace and goodwill to all his associates and his former wife, wishing for each one health, happiness, promotion and all the blessings of life. That short-circuit of guilt and inferiority had been unearthed and poise, peace and harmony now reign supreme. Love is the fulfilling of the law, and he knows now that "the ship that comes home to my brother comes home to me." His daughter, whom he had not seen in twenty years, recently came to visit him and there was a joyous reunion. Love is the fulfilling of the law.

POINTS TO REMEMBER

1. Many people are carrying excess burdens such as grief, resentment, self-condemnation and hostility. These are mental poisons that rob you of vitality, enthusiasm, and energy and debilitate the entire organism. Learn to cast off these burdens by opening your mind and heart to the influx of Cosmic Energy and Divine Love, which dissolves everything unlike itself.

2. A woman who hated her husband compensated by putting on excess aprons of flesh in order to become repulsive to men. She eventually realized that all hatred is self-hatred and that she was actually poisoning herself. She dissolved the lie and set her husband free, wishing for him all the blessings of life. Having forgiven herself,

she decreed to her subconscious every night prior to sleep that she weighed 120 pounds. Her subconscious freed her from the desire for amylaceous and fatty foods. Her beauty, grace and charm returned.

3. When you have a definite aim, goal or vision in life, you will discover that the Cosmic Energizer will flow on your behalf, vitalizing your whole being. Creative ideas and inspiration will flow and all doors will be opened to you, bringing about a fulfillment of your dream.

4. Men block their promotion, growth and expansion by criticizing and condemning others. What they fail to see is that when you condemn, criticize, demean and belittle others, you, being the thinker, are actually creating all these qualities within yourself. Also, you are actually trying to drag others down to your own low estimate of yourself. Men tend to project on to others the shortcomings, inadequacies and inferiorities within themselves. It is not what others say or do, it is our thought about it that matters. The solution is to exalt God in the midst of yourself and to salute the Divinity in others, wishing for them prosperity, promotion and all the blessings of life. Do this regularly and systematically until it becomes a habit, and you will find the peace that passeth understanding.

5. A secretary was placing herself in a mental house of bondage by giving power to other girls to hurt her and was burning up her own vital energy, resulting in nervousness and insomnia. She identified herself with the Divine Presence within her and looked upon this Supreme Power as her guide, counsellor, paymaster, adjustor

and source of all blessings. At the same time, she silently saluted the Divinity in all the other girls, affirming, "God loves you and cares for you." She found peace in this changing world. She changed inside, and the outside world changed in the image and likeness of her contemplation.

6. Paul says:—*Faith which worketh by love* (Galatians 5:6). This love is not a Hollywood confection or a sentiment. It means an outreaching of the heart, an emanation of goodwill to all. It is that inner feeling of faith and confidence which enables you to fulfill your dreams regardless of the criticism or ridicule of the world. It also means that regardless of the vilification, hostility or jealousy of others, you tenaciously keep on until the day breaks and the shadows flee away. It is essential that you maintain cordiality, amiability and goodwill to all people everywhere for although as Paul says, you have the faith that moves mountains, and you lack love, you are as nothing. Faith works by love.

7. A woman living in a retirement home, bitter, hostile and disillusioned with her children who never communicated with her, decided to become a focal point for the Cosmic Energizer and claimed that It was flowing through her as currents of life, love, truth, abundance and security. She made a habit of giving thanks for God's riches flowing freely to her and began to live by the law of love, wishing for everyone all the blessings of life. Wonders began to happen in her life. Her daughter phoned her out of the blue and invited her to travel to Europe for six weeks. While there she met the man of

her dreams and married him, and they are now living the life more abundant in Spain. She learned to cast the burden on the God-Self within and become free.

8. Learn to forgive yourself first for harboring negative thoughts about yourself or anybody else. You can't give what you don't have. When you let the sunshine of God's love in to your soul, you can release to others the imprisoned splendor within you. Begin now to let the influx of Divine Love into your soul. Exalt God in the midst of you. When love enters in there is no room for resentment, ill will, jealousy or enmity. All are dissolved in the Light of God's Love.

9. A man was trying to exalt himself by tearing others down. This indicated his own inferiority, insecurity and sense of guilt which were unresolved. He was wasting his vital energy and had lost his grip on life. He learned that he was punishing himself and resolved his sense of guilt by forwarding $30,000, on the suggestion of his attorney, to his former wife and child, whom he had deserted twenty years previously. Self-condemnation is hell and self-forgiveness is heaven. There was a joyous reunion with his own daughter, and he found that love and goodwill wipe away all tears. He respects the Divinity within himself now, and what automatically follows from this is the conscious respect for the Divinity in all men. He knows now the truth of the ancients: The ship that comes home to my brother comes home to me.

5

How the Cosmic Energizer Can Bring You All Kinds of Blessings

EVERY MAN IS a son of God and every woman is a daughter of God, for there is but One Power, One Presence, One Cause and One Substance. Learn to tune in with the Cosmic Energizer, and as you do you will find yourself coming of age spiritually in your new capacity, functioning in terms of your Real Self.

Begin to claim that you are energized from On High and that you are doing all things through the God-Power within you, and you will find yourself ignited by the Cosmic Energizer and you will emit sparks—electrical energy and force that can actually be sensed and appreciated. Contacting the God-Self is like contacting high-tension wires. Results do ensue!

All life is largely an absorption of a power that you as yet do not know to be actually there. Before you, the dynamo, begin rotating there is only potential power as a possibility. But when you begin to move as a dynamic, magnetic personality ("dynamo"), you will soon emit sparks and generate power from the Source of all power. However, you must become a "self-starter." Some people only "come to life" in emergencies instead of making it a daily habit of abiding continually in the field of potential energy.

How She Discovered the Cosmic Energy

A frail woman weighing about 90 pounds told me that she had lifted a truck under which her husband was pinned and released him. Four men tried to lift the same truck some hours later and could not do so. Her power and energy were always there, and when she assumed it was there the Cosmic Energy responded.

Assumptions Become Concrete Realities

Churchill said our assumptions harden into facts. When chatting with a returned veteran from Vietnam, he said that when he was lost in the jungle at first he was fearful; then he sat down and said to himself: "I'm all right. God is here, too." He recalled that one time at home he had been lost in the mountains and had asked a man who was fishing in a stream the way back to the main highway. The man told him the way. He had assumed that the directions were correct and shortly found himself on the main highway. Likewise, he assumed God would guide him back to his battalion or to friendly hands. He began to walk, and in some hours he walked directly to the medics who took care of him.

Assumptions harden into facts and become objectified on the screen of space.

There Are Tremendous Possibilities Within You

God, the Living Spirit Almighty, dwells in you, and walks and talks in you. Lord Chesterfield said: "Some men live and die with all their greatness still within them." You are a Powerhouse dynamo, and you can release the hidden powers through the assumption of right ideas, feelings and attitudes of mind. God's potential must be increased through your dynamic action, or It will move on and away from you.

Believe in God that *is in you* (as a potential), ready to be released like Aladdin's genii. Let this Energy go through the blood vessels of your body by claiming boldly: "I am filled with the energy and wisdom of the Infinite One. It is coursing through my veins now." As you continue to do this, you will move dynamically toward health, wealth and vitality.

How She Experiences the Blessings of Life

A businesswoman with whom I had a long-distance conversation complained that her business, marital and home conditions were very bad and practically beyond her control. I pointed out to her that, on the contrary, she had control and dominion over her thoughts, feelings, actions and reactions, and that she must definitely assume responsibility for harmony, peace and happiness in her life.

On the phone I suggested that she open the Bible and read Ezekiel 34:26:—*There shall be showers of blessing.* I suggested that she enthrone that idea in her mind, and the idea being dynamic, she should listen to it with an inner ear. It would then penetrate her subconscious and release its energy.

This woman's life was dried up, like the soil that has been too long without rain. She was full of fear, resentment and hatred toward her husband and filled with a sense of defeatism. She said her first year in business had been a great success—beautiful and harmonious. She took credit for the first year's success. I pointed out, however, that she must also assume responsibility for her failures and discordant home life.

A few weeks passed by and I had a wonderful letter from her saying that she had begun to sing to herself: "There shall be showers of blessings for me." She got lost in the idea, and it found its way into her subconscious. From then on everything changed: Business picked up; there were new customers and a promotion for her husband. She is now possessed with a new zest for living. As she began to sing the song of triumph to herself, she dissolved all the bitterness and hostility and the Cosmic Energizer began to flow through her as harmony, health, peace and abundance.

FEAR BLOCKED HIS FLOW OF ENERGY

Recently I talked with a businessman who was afraid of the future, of devaluation of the dollar, of some dire malady and bankruptcy. I explained to him that he was blocking the flow of his potential energy and, consequently, becoming less effective in his work. There is no occasion for fear, for there is an antidote within him to cast out fear. The antidote is God within man. This Power is Supreme, Omnipotent, Omnipresent, and there is nothing to oppose the One Power, nothing to thwart It or vitiate It. I gave him a Bible verse containing these dynamic words:—*Be strong and of good courage; be not afraid, neither be thou dismayed: for the Lord thy God is with thee whithersoever thou goest* (Joshua 1:9).

He began to affirm frequently: "God, the Almighty One, is guiding me and directing me in all ways. His love surrounds me, enfolds me and encompasses me. This Power flows through me as harmony, strength, right action and Divine love." Whenever a fear thought came to his mind, he supplanted it immediately by affirming, "God loves me and cares for me."

He made a habit of this and found that by disciplining himself, the obsession of fear was dissipated and dissolved in the light of God's love. He realized that by persistent repetition of eternal verities, he caused the Power of the Infinite to be active and potent in his life. His fear has changed to faith in God and all things good. His new-found faith in the Infinite Presence and Power has created a channel in his mind, and from this groove all his other thoughts take their quality and color. Now all his thoughts are tinged with faith, confidence, love and goodwill. The Biblical verse I gave him saturated his mind and heart and healed him of all his fears.

How He Received More Power and Energy

Recently I conducted a class on the "Psychological and Spiritual Meaning of the Book of John" in the New Testament. I explained the meaning of the verse:—*But as many as received him, to them gave he power to become the sons of God . . .* (John 1:12). I explained that if any man opened his mind and heart to the influx of this Cosmic Energy and Power, he could do great things, and that his motto in life should be, "I can do marvelous and wonderful things through the God-Power which strengtheneth and guideth me."

A son of God means any man who realizes that God indwells him and that God is his Father, the Life-Principle, the progenitor or Father of all, for there is only One Creative Principle. Therefore, I said to believe that God is your silent partner, your guide, your paymaster, your trouble-shooter, your advisor, your source of supply and your instant and everlasting support at all times. "You came," as Wordsworth said, "trailing clouds of glory . . . from God which is our home."

One man at the end of the class session said to me that every morning he stood before the mirror and said out loud: "I am a son of God. Victory is mine, triumph is mine, success is mine, wealth is mine, harmony is mine. God is my partner. It is wonderful!" The class lasted five weeks. He practiced this technique every morning. On the third week, as a complete surprise, he was asked by the governing board of his corporation to be president of the company with a salary of $50,000 plus expenses. New ideas came to him continuously, and in one instance he saved the company $100,000 due to an intuitive voice which told him how to solve the problem.

This man began to realize the tremendous power and wisdom lying dormant within him and called upon It, and he felt the response. He said to me, "I know now that nothing in life can defeat me. I know how to tap the Power."

SHE SAID, "I'M SO RELIGIOUS. WHAT IS WRONG?"

Recently a woman said to me, "I have great faith in my religion. I believe in the Commandments, the Golden Rule, and in the tenets of my church; yet, I am not successful, I can't make ends meet, and I am frustrated and unhappy in my work. I pray and get no answer."

The reason for all this was that her religion was purely formal. She was giving lip service to the doctrines and tenets of her church. While she was conventionally good, she expected reverses, was full of self-condemnation, was resentful of associates in business, and believed that God punishes people. She subscribed intellectually to the doctrines, creed and dogmas of the church. This was her formal belief, all of which was superficial.

I explained to her that the only thing that really mattered was the belief she held deep down in her heart—her emotional espousals, her fears and deep-seated convictions. Religion is that mental attitude which binds you. Her dominant idea was condemnation of herself. The idea that binds you is your real religion. Your dominant belief about yourself, life and God is your real religion. Your subconscious assumptions, convictions and beliefs dictate and control all your conscious action. In other words, your religion is your relationship with God.

This woman practiced the mirror treatment by standing in front of the mirror every morning about five minutes, affirming out loud and with deep feeling: "I am a daughter of the Infinite. God loves me and cares for me. I exalt God in the midst of me. I am whole, perfect, loving, harmonious. I am inspired from On High. God works wonders through me." Any time the thought of self-condemnation or resentment came to her, she immediately chopped its head off by reminding herself, "God loves me and cares for me."

Within a month's time she married a successful scientist, has now a new concept of herself and has fallen madly in love with the great truths of life. Truly, wonders happen as you pray.

POINTS TO REMEMBER

1. Every man is a son of God and every woman is a daughter of God, for there is but One Power, Presence, Cause and Substance. Begin now to claim that you can do all things through the God-Power that strengthens you.

2. All life is an assumption of power, which as yet you do not know to be actually there. Assume the power exists and you will soon emit sparks and generate power from On High.

3. A frail and physically weak woman, seeing her husband pinned under a truck, lifted it up and freed him. Subsequently, four men could not lift the truck. She assumed the power was there and the Cosmic Energizer responded.

4. Churchill said that our assumptions harden into "faith." A veteran implicitly assumed that there was a guiding principle that would lead him out of the jungle, and he was Divinely led every step of the way and eventually found himself in the arms of his comrades.

5. You are a powerhouse and you can release the hidden powers through the assumption of right ideas, feelings and attitudes of mind. Claim boldly that you are filled with the Energy and Wisdom of the Infinite and that this power is now coursing through your veins and arteries. You will feel the influx of Energy from On High.

6. A woman who was despondent, gloomy and in financial straits enthroned an idea: "There shall be showers of blessings." The idea captivated her mind, generating tremendous energy and power, which transformed her life financially and socially, resulting in marital harmony and prosperity.

7. Fear was blocking the flow of the Cosmic Energizer, and one man began to use the great antidote—God within him. He enthroned in his mind this great truth: *Be strong and of good courage; be not afraid, neither be thou dismayed: for the Lord thy God is with thee whithersoever thou goest* (Joshua 1:9). Whenever fear came to his mind, he supplemented the thought with "God loves me and cares for me." He made a habit of this and succeeded in casting out fear. When fear knocks at the door of his mind, faith in God opens the door and there is no one there.

8. A man began to claim, feel and believe that God was his silent partner, guide, counsellor, paymaster, adjustor and trouble-shooter. He gave himself the mirror treatment and affirmed before the mirror every morning: "Victory is mine, triumph is mine, success is mine, wealth is mine. God is my partner. It is wonderful!" He became president of his company and fabulous ideas welled up from his depths, saving and making money for his organization.

9. She said she was religious but experienced lack and limitation. True religion, however, is really of the heart, or the subconscious. It is what you sincerely believe deep down in your heart that is made manifest in your life. Your nominal belief, or theoretical assent to certain

creeds, dogmas, rules and regulations is thinking in the head; but it is the thinking in your heart, or subconscious, that matters. Your dominant belief is your real religion. Believe in the goodness of God in the land of the living. Believe in the guidance of God and the love of God. Believe in the abundance and riches of the Infinite, and God will wipe away all tears from your eyes and there will be no more weeping.

6

How the Cosmic Energizer Can Work Miracles of Healing for You

RECORDS OF MAN's mental and physical illnesses as recorded in the Bible have reoccurred from time immemorial up to the present moment. You may see the conditions and symptoms of diseases described in the Bible in almost any hospital in the country. It is true, of course, that the diseases described today have scientific names derived from medical terminology.

However, all over the world men and women of various religious beliefs are awakening to the tremendous therapeutic results following the application of mental and spiritual laws. In the fields of medicine, psychiatry, psychology and other related fields, evidence is being adduced and articles written on mental and emotional conflicts as the underlying cause of all kinds of destructive disease.

THE COSMIC ENERGIZER, THE INFINITE HEALING PRESENCE, IS THE BASIS OF ALL HEALING

All healing takes place according to the belief of the individual. The subconscious mind is the creative faculty within us and manifests whatever the conscious mind impresses upon it; the conscious mind impresses its thought upon it; the thought is the expression of the belief; hence, whatever is impressed on the subconscious mind, the latter reproduces according to our belief. The wrong belief, which externalizes as sickness, is the belief that some secondary cause, which is only a condition, is a primary cause.

SHE CHANGED HER BELIEF AND HAD A MIRACULOUS HEALING

I had a most interesting talk a few days ago with a taxi driver. He told me that his mother was in the habit of saying, "I suppose one of these days I will get arthritis and be crippled like my mother and grandmother." He said that as a boy he thought nothing of it, until the day came when his mother actually became crippled with arthritis and was hospitalized.

Her son took her a copy of *The Power of Your Subconscious Mind** and said to her, "Mother, read this." She did so, at the same time saying to him, "I want you to pray for me." The physician in attendance told this young man that his mother would have to use a wheelchair for the rest of her life.

Following the reading of the book and the constructive suggestions of her son, however, she realized what had caused her arthritic condition—her subconscious mind. Being impersonal, it had accepted her negative statement which she had repeated over and over again: "I suppose I will get arthritis just like my mother and grandmother." Actually, she realized she had brought it on herself, as the subconscious takes you literally.

The Power of Your Subconscious Mind by Dr. Joseph Murphy. Prentice-Hall, Inc., Englewood Cliffs, N.J., 1963.

Her New Attitude Changed Everything

She realized that she had to reverse her thinking; accordingly, at my suggestion, several times a day she reiterated certain truths that her subconscious accepted. I wrote out the following prayer for her: "The Living Spirit within me is the Infinite Healing Presence. I am now planting the idea of wholeness, vitality and perfect health in my subconscious mind. Divine love flows through me, dissolving everything unlike Itself. Divine peace fills my soul. The vitality and intelligence of the Infinite Healing Presence permeates and penetrates down to my innermost depths in my subconscious mind. I know that every time I use this prayer I am strengthening my subconscious mind in its hold on this new belief until I again walk freely and joyously."

Her son continued to pray for his mother in a similar way, and though she came home using a wheelchair, in a month's time she became completely healed and now comes every Sunday to hear me at the Wilshire Ebell Theatre in Los Angeles.

How She Released the Cosmic Energizer's Healing Power

Some months ago, I had the opportunity to observe the wonderful results of a mother who had the faith to believe in the infinite healing presence within her subconscious mind. She brought her 5-year-old son to see me. He seemed to be an exceptionally fine, healthy boy, but the mother said that he had been suffering from severe asthmatic attacks, and that the medicine he was taking did not always suppress the attacks. The boy's father had passed on shortly after he was born, and the asthmatic condition had come on about six months previous to seeing me.

I told her that she could again see her boy whole and perfect. St. Augustine said, "For what is faith unless it is to believe what you do not see?" She set herself the task of demonstrating her faith in the Cosmic Energizer. This mother had a wonderful knowledge of mental and spiritual laws and said to me, "I know that my prayer of faith, though denied by the evidence of my senses, if persevered in, will be deposited in my subconscious mind and come to pass."

Three or four times a day, she became still and quiet, and in her imagination she pictured her boy in front of her saying, "Mom, God healed me. I feel wonderful." She persisted in this mental image, and at the end of a month the boy was completely free from the paroxysmal attacks of asthma. Her favorite quotation is:—*For we walk by faith, not by sight* (II Corinthians 5:7). She disciplined her mind and knew that her constructive thought-image and the invisible mold created by her in her mind would be subjectified and come to pass.

You Can Practice the Absent Healing Technique

The Cosmic Energizer is the Life-Principle which animates all people. For example, if your brother is in a foreign country and you wish to pray for him, you must remember that there is no hard and fast line of demarcation between personalities, as subjectively we are all one. When you think of your loved one, there is no time or space in your subconscious mind; therefore, he picks up your thought of wholeness, beauty, vitality and love, and these qualities are resurrected within him.

The action is that of your conscious mind towards your loved one or friend, and his willingness to receive this is called being in rapport with the other person. The Cosmic Energizer, or the Living Spirit (God), is present in its entirety at every point simultaneously. When you give absent treatment or pray for another person who is not present objectively, you can decree wholeness and vitality to the subconscious mind of the sick friend as though it were your own, and according to your belief and conviction, results will follow.

—*For as he thinketh in his heart, so is he . . .* (Proverbs 23:7).

Miraculous Healing of a Child Dying with Fever

While writing this chapter, I received a long distance phone call from Georgia. The woman who had called me said that her child was dying; that the medicine given did not reduce the fever, and that there seemed to be no hope.

I explained to her that the child (6 years old) would respond to her faith and confidence in the Infinite Healing Presence within the child. This mother, at my suggestion, was to withdraw her thought from the contemplation of fever and symptoms and from the corporeal personality altogether, and then to affirm knowingly and feelingly: "The Cosmic Energizer—the Living Spirit Almighty—is the life of my child. God's river of peace saturates her whole being. God's love fills her soul. The vitalizing, healing, harmonizing power of God is made manifest in her mind and body now. The vitality and intelligence of God are resurrected now, and I give thanks."

She repeated this prayer for about one-half hour over and over again, knowing that the subconscious mind of her child would become thoroughly imbued with the realization of its own healing power and that health would be restored. At the end of one-half hour, the child's temperature became normal, and the medical doctor said to the mother, "A Higher Power did this." The child asked to play with her dog and also for something to eat.

—*Let the weak say, I am strong* (Joel 3:10).

Steps in Mental and Spiritual Healing

The first step you must take is to refuse to be afraid of the manifest conditions from this very moment. The second step is to come to the realization that the condition is but the product of negative thinking, which will have no power to continue its existence. The third step is to exalt the healing power of the Cosmic Energizer within the person.

This will stop the production of all toxins in you or the person you are praying for. Pronounce the condition false; lift the person up in your mind, seeing the sick person as he ought to be—happy, joyous and free. Live in the embodiment of your desire, and the word (your thought and feeling) will be made manifest.

How a Minister Released the Healing Power

Recently I talked with a minister from New York City, who informed me that he gets wonderful results by using one of

my books, *Miracle of Mind Dynamics.** His wife had tubercu-
losis and was not responding to therapy or to the climate in
Tucson, Arizona, where she had spent an entire summer.

This minister friend of mine selected a passage from the
Bible:—*Jesus lifted up his eyes, and said, Father, I thank thee that
thou hast heard me. And I knew, that thou hearest me always* . . .
(John 11:41-42).

Three or four times a day, he would calm his mind, relax
and let go. Then he would imagine that he was talking to the
Invisible Healing Presence within, and his inner speech was,
"Thank you, Father, for my wife's miraculous healing." He
repeated this over and over again until his mind was saturated with the feeling of thankfulness.

His wife continued the same technique. At the end of a
month the sputum and all other tests were completely negative. As they lifted up their minds and hearts to the Infinite
Healing Presence, they released the healing power. Their inner speech agreed with their aim. Ouspensky had a favorite
saying, which was that your inner speech (your inner conversation, your silent thought) must agree with your aim or
desire in life. It is your inner speech or conversation that is
always made manifest.

In this instance, their inner speech agreed with their aims
of wholeness, beauty and perfection. *And I, if I be lifted up
from the earth* (the condition, symptom or problem), *will draw
all men* (manifestations) *unto me* (John 12:32).

---

*Miracle of Mind Dynamics by Dr. Joseph Murphy, Prentice-Hall, Inc., Englewood
Cliffs, N.J., 1964.

THE MASTER KEY TO SPIRITUAL HEALING

The ideal way to practice spiritual mind healing is to completely withdraw all thought from symptoms and from the corporeal condition altogether, and to think of the person for whom you are praying as a purely spiritual being; in other words, identify with the Spirit or Cosmic Energizer within him, and then claim that what is true of the Spirit is true of the person you are trying to help.

In this technique, you realize that the Spirit (God) is omnipotent and entirely free from subjection to any condition. You affirm that the patient is now expressing the vitality, intelligence, wholeness and power that constitute the Spirit. The patient is open and receptive to your affirmations of truth, and his subconscious mind becomes charged with the constructive spiritual thoughts of the healer. Wholeness, vitality and strength are resurrected, and health is substituted for sickness.

HOW HE WAS SNATCHED FROM DEATH'S DOOR

A woman came to see me a few months ago, saying that her husband was afflicted with delirium tremens, usually called the DT's. His heart was fibrillating and he was also hallucinating. The doctor said his death was only a matter of hours. She asked me to go with her to the hospital, as he was asking for me and had been listening to my radio programs on KIEV every morning.

He was under sedation of morphine, but was nevertheless coherent and rational. He was a chronic alcoholic and during the bedside conference recited all the crimes he had committed, which were many. He said, "I'm at the end of my rope. I'm dying. Will I go to hell?" He had old-fashioned religious ideas, even though he had discontinued going to any church.

I explained to him that the Life-Principle (God) never condemns; that all judgment is given to the son, which means our mind, and that we judge ourselves and make our own hell (restriction, bondage) and own heaven (peace, harmony, good health, etc.). I further explained to him that all he had to do was to forgive himself for all his past transgressions and to resolve not to commit them again; furthermore, he could join with me now and we would release all those for whom he had a grudge or resentment as well as all those who had passed over into the next dimension. I told him that perfunctory prayer is not the answer, but, instead, a real change of heart where, from the depths of himself, he had to really wish for all those for whom he had past resentments to have health, happiness, peace and all the blessings of life.

He named about ten persons, some in the next dimension sent there by himself, and we began to pour out God's love, peace, joy and all the blessings of life upon each one. Suddenly he seemed radiant and happy. The reason for this was that he now had a deep, inner faith that there was no power up there which was going to punish him.

He felt that he was on the right side of God and that all was forgiven. He relaxed and was ready for what he termed "Heaven." The psychiatrist and nurse noted a remarkable physical improvement, and the new prognosis was that he would live. In a few days he was whole and perfect. The man is now vital, alive and bubbling over with enthusiasm.

His forgiveness of himself and others, his relaxed attitude, and his surrender to God immediately released his mind and body from the presence of pain, fear, guilt and hatred. His body responded in a miraculous manner to his new mental attitude. His inner sense of freedom and peace of mind released the healing power of the Cosmic Energizer, and he was a new man in God. He realized that self-condemnation is hell, and that self-forgiveness is heaven—a mind at peace.

How the Law of Mind Forgives and Heals

The law of your subconscious mind has nothing to do with goodness, badness, creeds, dogmas or religious persuasions. The law is impersonal, for God is no respecter of persons. The sun shines upon the unjust as it does upon the just. The rain falls on the good and the evil. There is no morality in the law of your mind. It is always impartial, impersonal and neutral. Morality depends on your motivation and how you use the law of mind. Your thought carries its own reward. Your idea, desire, plan or purpose is good or bad depending on the nature of the desire or plan itself. Choose good and good follows.

You can bring your desire to pass without hurting a hair of a living being in this world. Paul says that—*Love is the fulfilling of the law* (Romans 13:10). This means that when you think right, feel right, act right and do right you have used the law constructively and you will have goodwill toward all. This outreaching of your heart toward others will cause them to react in a similar manner toward you.

Forgiveness and Healing

In the Bible is the statement that you are to forgive—*Until seventy times seven* (Matthew 18:22). This is a figurative expression, which means a thousand times a day, if necessary, or a constant spirit of forgiveness. Your mind is a principle, and when you use the principle in the right way, it has no grudge against you. For example, if you used the principles of mathematics, chemistry or electricity in an ignorant or erroneous way, these same principles would not hurt you, condemn you or punish you when you began to use them in the right way. A new beginning is a new end.

The Life-Principle never condemns or punishes you. Actually, you punish yourself by misuse of the law and by negative thinking. The marvelous and wonderful truth to learn is that you forgive yourself on the basis of a scientific mental law which is that your subconscious mind automatically reverses its action toward you when you begin to think the right way. It makes no difference whether you are an alcoholic, dope fiend, mugger, thief, rapist, murderer or sadist; the law of your subconscious does not hold any grudge against you, neither does it react negatively any more once you have made a sincere decision to become a transformed man and to practice and live the truths of God, which are the same yesterday, today and forever.

All our derelictions, sins, errors, crimes, hostilities and resentments are wiped out when we change our hearts and acknowledge that the love and harmony of God reign supreme in our lives. When Divine love, Divine harmony and Divine peace dominate your mind and heart, the law of your subconscious, being compulsive, will compel you to express the qualities and attributes of God, and all your ways will be ways of pleasantness and all your paths will lead to peace.

—*But this one thing I do, forgetting those things which are behind, and reaching forth unto those things which are before, I press toward the mark* . . . (Philippians 3:13-14).

POINTS TO REMEMBER

1. All over the world today men and women of various religious beliefs are awakening to the tremendous therapeutic results following the application of mental and spiritual laws.

2. All healings take place according to the belief of the individual or that of his doctor or practitioner. The subconscious mind is the creative medium, and the healer of the body. Whatever the conscious mind impresses on the subconscious, the latter faithfully reproduces.

3. The mother of a taxi driver began to read *The Power of Your Subconscious Mind** and realized that she had been constantly fearing and expecting to be crippled with arthritis because her mother and grandmother had been afflicted with this disease. She changed her attitude and began to affirm regularly, systematically and conscientiously that the Cosmic Energizer within her, which is the Infinite Healing Presence, was flowing through her as harmony, vitality, and wholeness, and

---

The Power of Your Subconscious Mind by Dr. Joseph Murphy, Prentice-Hall, Inc., Englewood Cliffs, N.J., 1963.

that she was energized and transformed by the Healing Presence. She also pictured herself as walking and doing all the things she would do were she whole and perfect. Her son kept praying for her, also, claiming that Divine love, peace and harmony saturated the mind and heart of his mother. His mental image, which he constantly viewed, was his mother at home, vital, alive and quickened by the Spirit. His image agreed with his affirmation, and the so-called miracle happened: All the calcareous deposits were dissolved and she walks freely and joyously now.

4. A mother whose 5-year-old son had paroxysmal attacks of asthma, and whose medicine did not always succeed in suppressing them, decided to call on the Infinite Healing Presence within her and the boy. Several times a day she sat still, immobilized her attention, and in a passive, receptive frame of mind, imagined her little boy saying to her, "Mom, God healed me. I feel wonderful." She did this over and over again until she felt the naturalness and reality of it all. It was a vivid, realistic drama in her mind. At the end of a month's time he was completely free and bubbling over with enthusiasm.

5. The Cosmic Energizer is the Life-Principle, or Infinite Healing Presence, which animates all people. If you wish to pray for a friend or relative thousands of miles away, there is no time or space in mind. Spirit is omnipresent, and if you wish to help your friend, go within yourself and contemplate the wholeness, beauty, vitality, intelligence and power of the Infinite and claim that what is true of God is true of your friend. Do this until you

become quiet and relaxed and feel that that is all you can do for the present. Later on, when you feel led to pray, repeat the prayer process as if you were doing it for the first time. Each time you are penetrating deeper into your subconscious mind, as well as that of your friend, and he will experience a resurrection of what you feel and believe.

6. A mother whose child was dying of fever and who failed to respond to medication, withdrew all thought of fever and bodily conditions. She sat down by the child and affirmed with faith and confidence: "God's river of peace saturates the whole being of my child. The vitalizing, healing, harmonizing power of God is made manifest in her mind and body now." She continued for about one-half hour, and the child's temperature became normal. She asked for food and her dog to play with. The subconscious mind of the child was impregnated with the truths affirmed by the mother, and immediate results followed.

7. The first step in mental and spiritual healing is not to be afraid of disease or condition. The second step is to come to the conclusion that the condition is but a product of negative thinking, which will have no power to continue its existence. The third step is to exalt the healing power of the Cosmic Energizer within. This attitude of mind will stop the production of all toxins in you or in the person for whom you are praying.

8. A minister brought about a wonderful healing of his wife's tubercular condition by meditating on one of the verses of the Bible and reiterating it over and over again until it became embodied in his subconscious mind and

that of his wife. He turned within as if addressing the Infinite Presence and affirmed: "*Father, I thank thee that thou hast heard me. And I knew that thou hearest me always* . . . (John 11:41-42)*.*" He kept on thanking the Infinite for his wife's miraculous healing, knowing that the grateful heart is always close to God. A complete healing of the tubercular condition took place.

9. The master key to spiritual healing is to refrain from thinking of symptoms and conditions, but to think of the Living Spirit within, which is the God Presence, and then to affirm that the love, peace, harmony, joy, wholeness, vitality and intelligence of the Cosmic Energizer animates, sustains, restores and heals the person for whom you pray. You should also imagine the person as the person ought to be—happy, joyous, whole, vital and in perfect condition. Your mental image must always agree with your affirmation. You can pray this way as often as you deem necessary, and according to your faith will you see results.

10. An alcoholic felt guilty and feared death. When it was explained to him that he creates his own heaven and hell, he felt relieved. He learned the law of forgiveness and realized that there was no one punishing him but himself, and that the grudges, peeves and resentments he harbored were poisoning himself because whatever he was thinking about others, he was creating in his own life, since thought is creative. He decided to forgive himself and others, and he meant it. Love came into his soul and peace into his mind. He felt he was on the right side of God and that all was forgiven. A remarkable healing

followed, and he left the hospital in a few days. He is a transformed man today. He discovered that self-forgiveness is heaven (mind at peace) and self-condemnation is hell (restriction and bondage).

11. The law of forgiveness is a scientific law of mind. Your mind is a principle, and the minute you begin to use it the right way, there is an automatic response of your subconscious mind to correspond with your conscious direction and contemplation. This is why you read in the 100th Psalm:—*His mercy is everlasting; and his truth endureth to all generations* (Psalm 100:5). The principles of chemistry, mathematics, electricity, etc. hold no grudges against you because you misused them. The minute you use these principles in the right way, right results follow. This is why even murderers, as well as alcoholics, thieves, dope addicts and sex fiends who have an intense desire to become new men in God, discover that the past is forgotten and remembered no more the minute they begin to fill their subconscious with the truths of God. Perfunctory prayer won't do this, but when a real inner transformation takes place and you possess a hunger and thirst to do the right thing, then this seeming miracle takes place. A new beginning is a new end.

12. *Forgive until seventy times seven* is a figurative, Biblical expression, which means your life should be dominated by a constant attitude of forgiving, or giving for. Continue supplanting negative thoughts with constructive, harmonious thoughts and then you are constantly forgiving yourself. Your thoughts about another are also your thoughts about yourself. You are the only thinker

in your world, and your thought is definitely creative. You and you alone are responsible for the way you think. Whatever you think or wish for another, you are creating in your own body, experiences, conditions and events. It behooves you to forgive *seventy times seven*.

13. All our shortcomings and derelictions are completely forgiven when we become dominated by Divine love, harmony and peace; then the law of our subconscious responds accordingly, and since the law of our mind is compulsive, we find ourselves compelled to ways of pleasantness and to paths of peace.—*His mercy is everlasting; and his truth endureth to all generations* (Psalm 100:5).

7

How the Cosmic Energizer Can Change Your Life

IN MY EXPERIENCE extending over a great many years, I have found that the reason so many people do not get ahead is that they feel guilty about events and experiences earlier in their lives, and that self-criticism and self-condemnation block the flow of the Cosmic Energizer in their pursuit of happiness.

I have also discovered that those men and women who have come to a decision to forgive themselves and others invariably blossom forth in a wonderful way and have begun to lead what I like to call charmed lives. Everything they sincerely desire to accomplish comes to fruition in Divine Order. Self-condemnation brings failure and misery. Self-forgiveness brings happiness, peace and triumphant living.

UNDERSTAND THE WORD "SIN"

The word *sin* is from a Greek word meaning to miss the mark. When the Greek archers failed to hit the bull's eye, it was said that they had sinned, or had missed the mark. Your goal, desire, objective or ideal is the mark for which you are aiming. Failure to reach your goal or to attain your objective is to sin. You are really sinning when you fail to express health, wealth, peace of mind and true expression.

How She Forgave Herself and Found Happiness

Recently a young woman from Georgia came to Los Angeles and accepted a good position with the government. In talking with her, I found that she was very shy, timid and somewhat introspective. She complained that there were no men where she worked and that she wanted to meet the right man and marry him. She wanted a home and to love and be loved. This young woman was sinning in the true meaning of the word because she failed to realize her desire in life.

She Reversed Her Attitude

At my suggestion she began to feel wanted, needed and appreciated. Frequently during the day she would silently affirm: "I am wanted, needed, loved, cared for and appreciated." She began to imagine that she was being invited by a wonderful man to dine in the best restaurants, and that she was being escorted by him to concerts, movies and operas. She wrote down on a memo pad all her desires. Frequently during the day she would go over this list, knowing that gradually all her requests would become engraved in her subconscious mind and would come to pass.

She attended one of my classes which I gave in Costa Mesa and there met a wonderful engineer, who fell in love with her. He took her to the best restaurants in town and to many theatrical productions. He presented her with a new automobile as a prenuptial gift, and the author had the pleasure of performing the marriage ceremony.

The deeper currents of her mind responded to her disciplined imagination and fulfilled her heart's desire in Divine order. She is now leading a happy and charmed life full of wonders. The word *forgive* means to give for. She gave herself the mood of fulfilled desire for the feeling of lack, loneliness and limitation. She hit the mark by realizing her goals in life and ceased to sin.

You Have the Power to Forgive Yourself

You have the power to forgive yourself for all the errors, shortcomings and mistakes of your past by deciding to change your thoughts and keep them changed. The moment you begin to think constructively, harmoniously, peacefully, and lovingly based on eternal truths which never change, your subconscious will immediately respond to your constructive thoughts and imagery; and the past will be forgotten and remembered no more. A new beginning is a new end.

There is no time or space in the mind-principle, and the minute you decide to transform your life by filling your subconscious with life-giving patterns, the Cosmic Energizer cleanses your subconscious and you become free. The Life-Principle (God) never punishes. We punish ourselves instead by negative thinking and the misuse of the laws of life. Ignorance is the only sin, and all the punishment and misery of the world is the result.

He Was Blocking the Flow of Energy

Recently I talked to a man who was poverty-stricken and who was also very jealous and envious of the wealth and success of those around him. He said that he had joined a certain religious group and was *saved*. However, he remained poor, sick and needy. Obviously, he had not forgiven himself. I explained to him that he must demonstrate his faith, as we are always demonstrating and manifesting that in which we believe.

I explained to him that God, the Living Spirit Almighty, the Life-Principle, was within him and that this Infinite Intelligence would respond to his call upon It. Accordingly, he began to affirm with understanding that "God is my instant and everlasting supply and support, meeting all my needs instantaneously at all times everywhere." When thoughts of lack came to his mind, he would immediately supplant the negative thoughts with his constant affirmation, "God is my instant and everlasting supply and support."

Gradually his mind became conditioned to the real Source of all things, and the Cosmic Energizer began to flow on his behalf, giving him new vitality, energy, creative ideas, and a new position with a wonderful income. The energy of the Infinite flows in response to the eternal truths of life. His latest comment to me was, "I have cast the spell of God around me, and it is wonderful!"

Your Power to Be, to Do and to Have

You have the capacity to embrace an idea, to induce the mood of it, and to weave it into the fabric of your mind through feeling. When you sense your oneness with your desire, the Cosmic Energizer moves on your behalf and brings your desire to pass. This is the creative law operating in you. Such knowledge works wonders in your life.

HOW A NEW IDEA TRANSFORMED HIS LIFE

Some time ago, I interviewed a man who had failed in business and who had lost considerable money in the stock market, which his family sorely needed. He told me that he had to repent. He was feeling depressed and was full of self-condemnation which, I explained to him, was one of the most destructive of human emotions. His mental attitude was sending psychic pus throughout his entire system, debilitating the entire organism and making him a sort of mental wreck.

I pointed out to him that the word *repent* means to change your thought along constructive lines and to keep it changed; and that to *forgive* means to identify yourself with your aim or ideal in life. He listened carefully and said to himself, "I can use this knowledge." He began to realize that all he had to do was to dwell on the idea of success and prosperity, and as he did so, the subjective power would compel him to do all things necessary to become a success.

He began to meditate on the idea of success and prosperity prior to sleep each night. He would think of what success and prosperity meant to him, and that the Infinite was always successful in all undertakings, whether planet, tree or cosmos. He dwelt on the fact that the Infinite was within him and that he was born to win and to succeed in life, that he was successful in his relationships with others and in his chosen field, and that God's riches were constantly available to him.

He proceeded to impress his subconscious every night by affirming, "Success is mine now; wealth is mine now," repeating these words slowly and quietly for five or ten minutes before he went to sleep. In the sleepy state, the mind is more receptive and passive, and it is easier to impregnate the subconscious at that time.

The sequel is interesting. All of a sudden he felt a desire to take a course in public speaking and business management, plus additional courses in investments in the stock market. Today he is a very successful broker and has a wonderful income.

A Detective Leads a Charmed Life

Recently I gave some special lectures at the Church of Religious Science in Dallas, Texas. During a conversation with a detective in the hotel, he told me that he had been shot at at least twenty times, sometimes at close range, but that each time he had had a miraculous escape—either the gun had jammed or the gunman had misfired, and the bullet meant for him was always deflected from its mark.

His constant prayer, morning and night, is: "The whole armor of God surrounds me. I bear a charmed life. God is my hiding place and God encompasses me with songs of deliverance." This is his favorite prayer. By repetition, faith and expectancy he has engraved indelibly in his subconscious mind the conviction that God's love renders him impervious to all harm, and the Cosmic Energizer responds according to his belief.

TRANSFORM YOUR LIFE WITH MENTAL AND SPIRITUAL FOOD

Wisdom and understanding and the abundant life consist neither in eating meat nor in drinking coffee, nor yet in abstaining from eating and drinking either of these. You can lead an abstemious and ascetic life and be wise, strong, healthy and wealthy; or you can be married and the father of ten children, eat ham, drink coffee, and still be illumined, inspired, successful and prosperous.

Wisdom, which is an awareness of the presence of God within you, knows there is no particular virtue in living apart from the world and eating nuts, fruits, etc. Others enjoy life, eat what they like, and lead the abundant life, feasting on the truths of God and all things good. Man can eat the choicest food and yet be hungry for love, guidance, health and inspiration. Man is what he eats mentally and spiritually.

Feast on the goodness and the guidance of God in the land of the living. Saturate your mind with God's river of peace and love. Claim you are inspired from On High and make it a habit to pour out the sunshine of God's love on everyone. As you practice reiterating these truths your whole world, body, mind, business and home life will magically melt into the image and likeness of your contemplation. Why be concerned with nonessentials, with trivial things such as what you shall eat or what you shall drink? Why strain at gnats and swallow camels—mountains of ignorance, fear and superstition?

THE TRUTH THAT CHANGED HIS LIFE

While talking with a hard-working man, I learned that he was very conscientious, consistently followed the tenets of his church, tithed, gave to the poor, visited hospitals and was good and kind to his family, yet he suffered from all manner of troubles. His house was burned down, his two cars were stolen, he had had two major operations, he was accused falsely, and he found his wife unfaithful, giving birth to a child not his own, which proved to be a great shock to him.

I asked him a simple question: What is your concept of God?, knowing before I asked that the answer he would give would reveal the cause of all his troubles. He believed that God was a Being separate from himself, up in space somewhere, and that we are here to suffer; and that God sends sickness, pain and suffering to test us. He actually believed God was punishing him for sins he had committed years ago. Having such a weird, ignorant concept of God, he experienced the result of such a belief in the form of all kinds of difficulties and troubles.

I explained to him the thing that really matters is his real, subjective belief, the sincere belief deep in his heart, and that he would always demonstrate his deep-seated belief. That is why Dr. Phineas Parkhurst Quimby in 1848 said, "Man is belief expressed." This man, conceiving of a God afar off in the skies, had a God of caprice, possessing all the whims of a human being. With such a concept he was like the businessman who said to the writer, "I would be all right if God would leave me alone."

HIS NEW CONCEPT OF THE COSMIC ENERGIZER (GOD)

I suggested that he go back to the true concept of God given in Isaiah 9:6—*His name shall be called Wonderful, Counsellor, The mighty God, The everlasting Father, The Prince of Peace.*

Three times a day for about five or six minutes he began to affirm feelingly: "I exalt God in the midst of me, mighty to heal and restore me. I know God is absolute Bliss, absolute Harmony, Infinite Intelligence, Boundless Love, Omnipotent, Supreme, the only Presence, Power, Cause and Substance. I know God is Love, and Love can't do anything unloving. I know and believe that the will of God for me is a greater measure of joy, happiness, love, peace, success, harmony, perfect health and the life more abundant. I claim, feel and know that the vitality, tireless energy, wholeness, and beauty and joy of the Infinite animate and sustain me, and that God's love fills my soul. I give thanks for God's riches, which are forever active, forever present, unchanging and eternal."

This man had a wonderful voice, and every morning and evening he would sing these truths, knowing by frequent habitation of the mind that they would enter into his subconscious and become manifest. It has now been over three months since he started this prayer technique and his whole life has been transformed. His health is wonderful, he has remarried and entered into the spirit of forgiveness. He now believes implicitly in a God of Love. God's love has dissolved everything unlike Itself in his mind, body, business and home. Wonders happen as you pray in the right way.

POINTS TO REMEMBER

1. The sense of guilt holds many people back, as it blocks the flow of cosmic energy into their lives, robbing them of vitality, enthusiasm and expansion in life. Self-condemnation brings failure and misery; self-forgiveness brings joy, happiness and prosperity.

2. The word *sin* means to miss the mark. You are sinning in life when you fail to lead a full, happy, prosperous and successful life.

3. A shy, timid and fearful young woman was lonesome, frustrated and unhappy. She reversed her attitude and began to claim she was wanted, needed, appreciated and loved. She disciplined her imagination and began to imagine and feel she was being escorted to fashionable restaurants, theatres and musicals. She also prayed that she would attract the right man. The deeper currents of her mind brought all these things to pass in Divine order.

4. To forgive is to give for. You have the power to forgive yourself by changing your thoughts according to universal principles and keeping them changed. The moment you do this, there is an automatic response from your subconscious mind, and the past is forgotten and remembered no more. A new beginning is a new end.

5. You do not solve the problem of poverty or sickness by joining a church, a cult or a group of any kind. You must

demonstrate your faith. We are all manifesting in our lives what we really believe. Turn to the Source of all blessings and claim that God, the Cosmic Energizer, is your instant and everlasting supply and support at all times and you will get a response.

6. When you sense your oneness with your desire, the Cosmic Energizer will move on your behalf and bring your desire to pass.

7. The word *repent* means to change your thoughts and to think according to eternal verities—the truths which never change. A man focused his attention on two ideas prior to sleep: "success" and "wealth," repeating these two words to his subconscious, while lulling himself to sleep. He activated the latent power of his subconscious and went up the ladder of triumph and achievement along all lines.

8. A detective lives a charmed life through the constant use of this prayer: "The whole armor of God surrounds me. I bear a charmed life. God is my hiding place, and He encompasses me with songs of deliverance." By constant repetition he has impregnated his subconscious mind, and he is impervious to all harm.

9. You are what you eat mentally and spiritually. You can eat the choicest food and still be hungry for love, peace, harmony and health. God doesn't care whether you feast or fast. Feast on the truths of God, and whatever you eat physically will be transmuted into beauty, symmetry, order and proportion.

10. You can be very good from a conventional standpoint; you can observe the rules and regulations of your church

and be kind to your family; but you must remember, it is the belief deep down in your heart that is made manifest. If you believe that God is punishing you or sending sickness or disease, or that the will of God for you is something downright unpleasant, you will experience the result of your belief. Actually, you are punishing yourself, because you are belief expressed. Get a new concept of a God of love, and believe that God's will for you is something glorious, and magnificent, and something beyond your fondest dreams, and it will be done unto you as you believe. One man who had been suffering the tortures of the damned because of his false belief about God reversed his attitude and enthroned a God of love. He thereby transformed his whole life into one of harmony, health and peace.

8

How the Cosmic Energizer Can Bring Divine Protection for You

ALL OF US must realize that we are immersed and surrounded by an Infinite Presence which possesses the answers to all the difficulties and problems of the world, a Presence which is referred to as Omnipotence, Omniscience, Omnipresence and Omniaction, and which responds to the thoughts of man.

When we use the term *Omnipotence*, we are referring to all the power and energy in the entire universe, and this Power or Energy is within you. All of God is present at any point in the universe, and it makes no difference how many individuals the Energy is flowing through; there is always an inexhaustible supply, as we are dealing with the Infinite Source of all Energy.

You are the heir to all the Energy there is, for there are no divisions in Infinity. The word *individual* means indivisible, and Infinity cannot be divided or multiplied. All of Omnipotence is present whenever you are. You can consider yourself the recipient of all the riches, power and wisdom of the Infinite, and at the same time you deprive no one else of anything.

The Cosmic Energizer Is Omniscient

Another term ascribed to the Cosmic Energizer is Omniscience, which is all wisdom, that which knows all and sees all. This All Wise One created the whole world and the galaxies in space, and also created you. It knows all the processes and functions of your body. Being All Wisdom, only It knows the answer to any problem under the sun. When the astronauts call on the All Wise One within for the answers to go to Mars, Venus and other planets, flashes of illumination will come into their minds revealing the perfect plan and the know-how of accomplishment.

The Cosmic Energizer Is Omnipresent

Another term we use for the Cosmic Energizer is Omnipresence, which reveals Its presence everywhere. It is within you and all around you. The Psalmist says:—*Whither shall I go from thy spirit? or whither shall I flee from thy presence? If I ascend up into heaven, thou art there; if I make my bed in hell, behold, thou art there. If I take the wings of the morning, and dwell in the uttermost parts of the sea; Even there shall thy hand lead me, and thy right hand shall hold me* (Psalm 139:7-10).

The Cosmic Energizer Is Omniaction

Yet another term we use is Omniaction. Here we recognize that a Supreme Wisdom fashioned the entire universe and governs all cycles of time as well as rotation of earth and planets. We see principles and laws moving rhythmically, harmoniously and systematically governing the entire cosmos. We are dealing with a framework of tireless Energy and an amazing mathematical certitude. The Psalmist declared this when he wrote:—*The heavens declare the glory of God; and the firmament sheweth his handywork* (Psalm 19:1).

THE UNIVERSALITY OF THE PROTECTING PRESENCE

Our Bible and all the Bibles of the world teach us of an Indwelling Presence which enables all of us to receive the protection and guidance of a Cosmic Energizer, the Miracle Power of the Universe. People of all walks of life and of different creeds have become aware of this mystic power and have used metaphors and figurative language in describing its wonder-working power.

HE WAS SAVED FROM A FIERY FURNACE

During a recent trip to Mexico City, I met a man at the pyramids outside the city, and while conversing with him, he told me that during the Korean War, his plane had been fired upon and caught fire. It was, as he said, a blazing furnace. All he could think of was the words of the Psalmist:—*He shall cover thee with his feathers, and under his wings shalt thou trust . . .* (Psalm 91:4). He said a great sense of peace came over him, and he knew intuitively he would not be hurt or burned. It was an inner knowing; not a hair of his head was singed, and he parachuted to safety.

His faith in the Protective Presence of the Cosmic Energizer immunized him against all harm. He proved that in an altered state of consciousness or higher dimensions of thinking, fire does not burn.

You Can Protect Yourself Against All Harm

The Old Testament gives an account of the long trek of the Hebrews through the "wilderness." They were protected by a pillar of cloud by day and a pillar of fire by night. Fire in the Bible represents the fire of Spirit, or the Cosmic Energizer, which never ceases its life-giving, purifying glow.—*Our God is a consuming fire* (Hebrews 12:29).

Fire means that the intelligence of God revealed answers in dreams and in visions of the night. Night means darkness, sleeptime. The cloud represents meditation wherein we are immersed in thought in the Divine Presence, knowing that we are impervious to all harm, and are invulnerable and invincible. The cloud means that we feel and know we are surrounded by the sacred circle of God's eternal love and that we bear a charmed life.

Some years ago I visited the pyramids of Egypt, and a guide informed me that in ancient times when caravans traveled through the desert, a man on a camel would precede them holding a brazier in his hand filled with burning charcoal. The smoke ascending from it could be seen miles away, enabling stragglers to orient themselves and find their way. He said that at nighttime people who had fallen behind could see the sparks, which in Bible language might be referred to as a pillar of fire by night.

The pillar of fire also represents light, or the intelligence which wells up from your subconscious depths as a warning, a revelation, an answer or a solution to a perplexing problem.

THE LIGHT OF THE COSMIC ENERGIZER SAVED HER LIFE

In a recent newspaper article, there was the story of a major airline disaster where more than 89 people lost their lives. A girl phoned me from Burlington, Vermont, saying that she had been scheduled to fly back to Boston, her home town, on that airship, but during the previous night in a dream she saw the ship on fire and all the dead bodies, and I appeared to her, saying, "Cancel your flight," which she did. She had been in correspondence with me regarding a family problem, and I had been praying for her. My appearance were purely symbolic; her subconscious knew she would follow the instructions of her minister and, therefore, projected a thought-image in her sleep.

This was the fire (intelligence, light on problem) by night (sleep time, darkness). The Psalmist says:—*For so he giveth his beloved sleep* (Psalm 127:2). The Cosmic Energizer always points the way, like the column of smoke by day in the desert and the column of fire by night as the sparks fly upward. It is God's love watching over you.

THE COSMIC LIGHT SAVED HIM FROM BANKRUPTCY

I had a conference with a man in San Francisco recently, who told me how he had been protected from going bankrupt. He was doing a very good business but found himself in the red and could not account for it. He trusted his employees, who had been with him since the inception of his business.

He turned within and spoke to his Higher-Self as follows: "You are all-wise. You know all things. Reveal to me what is wrong. I know and believe the answer will come clearly into my conscious, reasoning mind." Nothing happened for a few days, and then on the fourth night he had a hunch, or deep feeling, to go back to the store prior to closing, and there he found two of his assistants loading their automobiles with cartons of such items as cigarettes, whiskey and razors. He dismissed them and installed his son as night manager, and his business prospered immediately. He added that had the stealing continued, he would have become bankrupt within six months. He called on the Cosmic Energizer within himself and received the answer.

How the Protecting Presence Saved His Leg

In the August 19, 1973, issue of the newspaper *The National Enquirer* there appeared an article by John South:

Comedian Dan Rowan Diagnoses Own Ailment Under Hypnosis— And Proves Doctors Wrong

The night before *Laugh-In* star Dan Rowan was to undergo surgery for suspected leg cancer, he was hypnotized by a doctor. The results were incredible.

While under hypnosis, Rowan—who had no medical training—conveyed that a strange growth on his right leg was a noncancerous buildup of dead tissue. The next day, exploratory surgery proved that Rowan's statements under hypnosis were amazingly accurate.

In an exclusive *Enquirer* interview, the suntanned mustachioed comedian revealed his startling success with hypnotism.

"Two years ago, specialists told me that a large swelling on my right thigh might be cancerous and that they would need to perform an exploratory operation.

"The doctors said there was a real danger that they would have to cut my leg off at the hip. Naturally, I was upset by that possibility and I called a friend of mine, Dr. Raymond LaScola.

"He can make fantastic diagnoses by communicating with the patient's mind through hypnotism."

Dr. LaScola, a Beverly Hills specialist in pediatrics and clinical hypnosis, told *The Enquirer:*

I put Dan into deep hypnosis and used a technique called indiomotor questioning. In my questions, I used complex medical terms that Dan couldn't have consciously been able to understand. Under hypnosis, your subconscious mind may not know medical terms, but it can reveal causes of ailments.

Dr. LaScola's questions to Rowan required only "yes" or "no" answers. A "yes" answer was indicated by Rowan lifting the index finger of his right hand. Raising his little finger meant "no" and lifting his thumb indicated he didn't know the answer.

"Under this deep hypnosis, Dan's subconscious mind moved his fingers in answer to my questions. Dan couldn't consciously tune in to his body, but his subconscious mind could.

"From Dan's answers I learned that the swelling was not malignant and I was able to pinpoint the exact cause.

The diagnosis was confirmed the next day after the operation by a surgeon."

Said Rowan: "From my answers, Dr. LaScola diagnosed that the swelling was a buildup of dead tissue caused by my daily injections of insulin.

"I'm a diabetic and I take insulin shots every morning and night. This buildup looks like a tiny growth, but it's not dangerous and it usually goes away on its own.

"It was a great relief. The next day before surgery, I told the surgeon that there was no way I was going to lose my leg and I told him what he would find inside my leg.

"On the operating table, the surgeon opened my leg down to the bone and found it was just the way Dr. LaScola diagnosed.

"I believe more doctors should look into hypnosis of their patients before operating. It can be tremendously beneficial—even if no one really knows why it works.

"I've always been a great believer in the strength of human mind. It's remarkable how it can control your body.

"As a matter of fact, I'm under self-hypnosis right now to deaden the pain of my twisted ankle. It should be painful, but I feel no pain at all because I've put myself under hypnosis."

The preceding article reveals the wisdom of your subconscious mind* which always seeks to heal, restore and protect you. The infinite intelligence of your subconscious mind

---

*See *The Power of Your Subconscious Mind* by Dr. Joseph Murphy, Prentice-Hall, Inc. Englewood Cliffs, N.J., 1963.

made your body from a cell and knows all the processes and functions of your body. Being all wise, It knows only the answer to any problem. The Bible says:—*He shall call upon me, and I will answer him*—(Psalm 91:15).

THE COSMIC ENERGIZER IS THE GREAT SCIENTIST

Einstein said: "God is a scientist, not a magician." Think of God as an Infinite Intelligence that is cognizant of all things, the creator of all electrons, atoms and all things in the universe. This Protecting Presence knows how to use every form of energy to heal, save, bless and prosper humanity. We must learn to recognize, believe and accept the truth that there is an Infinite Intelligence that guides, protects and watches over us according to spiritual laws which execute themselves. Recognize God as the Supreme Scientist of the Universe governing the cosmos by mathematical, immutable laws, the Infinite Intelligence and Infinite Mind that indwells all of us, giving us the ability to think, reason, imagine and initiate new inventions, discoveries, and enables us to tap the infinite reservoir of all wisdom and power, revealing undreamed-of spiritual power.

HOW AN INVISIBLE WRITER SAVED HIS LIFE

On a recent trip to Guadalajara, Mexico, a man who sat next to me on the plane who was a professor of medicine was also very interested in psychic phenomena. He had been visiting an old friend in Sylmar, a town in the valley adjacent to Los Angeles, when the recent earthquake hit the hardest in the

Los Angeles area. He was sitting at a desk writing an article for a medical journal, and on the table opposite him were some books and stationery. All of a sudden he saw the pencil writing with no hand guiding it. It wrote in Spanish, saying, "Get out of here at once; an earthquake is coming." He left immediately, and one-half hour later that house was demolished. He said, undoubtedly, he would have been killed if he stayed.

Here was an invisible energy and an intelligence using this energy. It gave intelligent instruction and direction. He looked upon this experience as the subjective intelligence of his subconscious mind operating the pencil and speaking to him in such a way that he would instantly obey.

Many times in Ireland, England and other countries, I have sat with four or five people around a table which no one is touching, and the table became levitated, lifted up in the air, floated around without hurting anybody, and finally came back to its original position. In this instance we had the exhibition of energy governed by intelligence.

Some say that energy is governed by a spirit in the next dimension. We must assume, however, that we are just as much spirit now as we shall ever become. We are spirits with physical bodies, through which we function on this three-dimensional plane. Our relatives and friends who have passed on are spirits functioning in a four-dimensional body, and there is no other difference. The energy that moved the pencil and wrote the message for the professor was nonphysical, and it might also be exhibited by those in the next dimension of life. It is the One Spirit (God) operating in all men who ever lived, who are living now and whoever will live.

TUNE IN WITH THE FREQUENCY OF THE PROTECTING PRESENCE

There is that within us which enables us to tune in to the "frequency" of Infinite Life, Infinite Love and Infinite Wisdom. As we turn to this Presence in reverence and veneration, every need will be supplied, every desire fulfilled in Divine order, and all our ways will be ways of pleasantness and paths of peace.

POINTS TO REMEMBER

1. All of us are immersed and surrounded by an Infinite Presence and Power which has the answers to all the difficulties and problems of the world.
2. This Cosmic Energizer is all powerful. It is the only Power there is, and this inexhaustible and almighty energy is concentrated at every point of space. The tremendous energy locked in an atom is the Power of Almighty God focused at that point.
3. This Cosmic Energizer is all-wise; It knows all and sees all. It created the universe and the galaxies in space and indwells each person. This Protecting Presence made your body from a cell and knows all the processes and functions of your body. It is the Infinite Healing Presence which restores and heals. This Protecting Presence and Cosmic Energizer is present at every moment of time and point of space. Omnipresence could be likened to radio waves, which enable a person in Beverly Hills,

California, to hear the same program at the same moment as someone in New York City. You can make instant contact by phone with a friend in Honolulu.

4. The entire cosmos is governed by a Supreme Intelligence operating according to immutable, changeless laws so that scientists, for example, can forecast the return of Haley's Comet to the split second. This Presence and Power governs all cycles of time and the rotation of the earth and other planets, indicating we are dealing with a framework of tireless energy.

5. All the religions of the world teach us of an Indwelling Presence which enables all of us to receive the protection and guidance of a Cosmic Energizer, the Miracle Power of the Universe.

6. A man in Mexico City cited an experience wherein his plane was fired upon in the Korean War and caught fire. He began to think of God's Protecting Presence and affirmed, "He shall cover thee with his feathers, and under his wings shalt thou trust." Not a hair of his head was singed, and he parachuted to safety. He proved that at higher levels of thinking fire does not burn man.

7. The ancient Hebrews said they were protected by a pillar of clouds by day and by a pillar of fire by night. This is symbolic language. The cloud means man in tune with the Infinite contemplating the protecting presence of God. Fire by night means that the infinite intelligence in the subconscious mind reveals answers and guidance through dreams and visions when sound asleep. The cloud represents meditation or frequent contact with

the Infinite during our daily activities, while we know we are watched over and protected by an Overshadowing Presence at all times.

8. A plane en route from Burlington to Boston hit a wall in Boston and 89 lives were lost. That same evening a girl from Burlington, Vermont, phoned me, saying that the previous night she had seen the plane on fire in a dream with dead bodies all around. She said that this author had appeared to her and said, "Cancel your flight," which she did. She was praying for guidance and protection, and the infinite intelligence of her subconscious responded. Its ways are past finding out.

9. In the August 1973 issue of *The National Enquirer* there appeared an article by John South about comedian Dan Rowan, who was about to undergo surgery for suspected leg cancer. He went to see Dr. Raymond LaScola, who is not only a Beverly Hills specialist in pediatrics, but also an expert medical hypnotist. He put Dan in deep hypnosis and then asked Dan's subconscious mind to reveal the cause of the ailment and its real nature. He discovered there was no malignancy and his subconscious pinpointed the exact cause: The swelling in his leg was caused by dead tissue due to insulin injections. The infinite intelligence in his subconscious mind[*] revealed the answer, and he saved his leg.

10. Einstein said: "God is a scientist, not a magician." Think of God as the Cosmic Energizer and an Infinite Intelligence that is cognizant of all things, the creator of all

---

[*]*The Power of Your Subconscious Mind* by Dr. Joseph Murphy, Prentice-Hall, Inc., Englewood Cliffs, N.J., 1963.

things visible and invisible. Recognize God as the Supreme Scientist of the Universe governing the entire cosmos by mathematical, immutable laws.

11. On a recent trip to Guadalajara, Mexico, I met a professor of medicine whose life was saved during a recent earthquake at Sylmar, where he was at that time visiting a close friend. While seated at his desk writing a medical article, a pencil on another table began to write rapidly, directed by some unseen intelligence. The writing was in Spanish, which he spoke fluently, and its English equivalent was, "Get out of here at once. An earthquake is coming." He looked upon this experience as the subjective intelligence of his subconscious mind operating the pencil and speaking to him in such a way that he would instantly obey.

12. We must learn to trust the Infinite Protecting Presence, which is all-wise, all-loving and the Source of our being, to guide and protect us, not by magic, but by spiritual laws which execute themselves.

9

How the Cosmic Energizer Is an Ever Present Help That Guides You Intuitively

THE BIBLE SAYS: —*God is our refuge and strength, a very present help in trouble* (Psalm 46:1). One of the most beautiful and soul-stirring prayers in all the Bible is the wonderful poem called the 46th Psalm. The verse with which this chapter starts is an inspired verse that will enable you to overcome any difficulty. It is the supreme Bible prayer that enables you to overcome fear and worry. This power is instantly available and can be controlled through your thought.

How She Received Instant Help Which Saved Her Life

I had a phone call yesterday from a young lady who attends my Sunday lectures and classes, stating that she had been riding in a car on the freeway with two other girls when a man in another car approached them in the same lane; there seemed to be an inevitable crash, and the driver was paralyzed with fear. She said with love, "God is an ever present help; God is our refuge." The man suddenly swerved to another lane and was hit by an oncoming truck. He was thrown from his car unconscious, but not seriously hurt. She said they were saved from what seemed to be certain death. The Psalmist says that God is and that He is our refuge, "a very present help in trouble."

How the Cosmic Energizer Worked a Miracle

I had a conference recently with an ex-Sergeant of the Army, who had returned from Vietnam. He told me of a fascinating and absorbing episode which had occurred during his tour of duty there. One afternoon when he was on patrol with his men they walked right into six Viet Cong soldiers, who immediately killed all five men in his patrol before they could lift their rifles. Obviously, the Viet Cong had seen them coming and had ambushed them.

The enemy soldiers looked straight at him but never spoke or indicated they saw him. They went through the pockets of his men and took papers, weapons, and all contents. He was amazed and could not understand it. He found his way back to his battalion and later wrote about his experience to his mother in Kentucky. She wrote back: "They did not see you, son. They could not see you or touch you, because I have prayed daily, 'My son will always be invisible to the enemy. God is his refuge and fortress.'"

This man's mother decreed constantly that her son would be invisible to the enemy and would be protected by God. This was communicated to her son's subconscious mind, which responded according to the impression or decree given. Every letter she wrote her son concluded with these words taken from the 46th Psalm: "God shall help you, and that right early."

Undoubtedly these letters and prayers written by his mother had a profound effect upon him and made a deep impression in his subconscious mind, which responded to her conviction of God's protection for him.

The Cosmic Energizer Reveals a Hidden Fortune

I recently gave a seminar in Oklahoma City on "The Secrets of the Subconscious" to a distinguished group of men and women interested in research on the powers of the subconscious. I had accepted some interviews in the hotel. A man of Greek extraction visited me and wanted to know how he could advance financially. He had been working for 35 years at odd jobs in Oklahoma City. Before he had come to America, his mother had given him what she called a talisman—a good luck piece to wear around his neck—stating that it would bring him lots of money. This man had had constant trouble making ends meet and had read books on the mind but had never applied what he read.

I asked to see the charm he was wearing, which he referred to as "that red stone." It seemed to me to be very valuable and I suggested that he go to a jeweler to have it appraised, which he did. Its value was $30,000. It was a ruby. For 35 years he had lived in want, unable to give his family the things they needed, and all because he was ignorant of the wealth around his neck.

The average man is unaware of the wealth within, as well as the wealth without. Seek and ye shall find. This man was seeking an answer and he found it. I gave him a simple formula to use frequently, explaining to him that as he applied it regularly, he would never want all the days of his life. He was to affirm two or three times a day for three or four minutes the following: "God is an ever present help and God's wealth is circulating freely in my life. There is always a tremendous surplus."

He understood that as he wrote this truth with his conscious mind in the inner recesses of his subconscious mind, the latter would respond and magnify his good exceedingly. Furthermore, he was never to finish a negative statement about finances. Whenever the thought came, "I can't pay that bill," he immediately reversed it, affirming, "God is my instant supply and support—that bill is paid in Divine order."

All transactions take place in the mind, and unless things are paid for and accepted mentally, one does not experience any result on the objective plane of life. You can't gain and lose except through your mind. Wealth is a thought-image in your mind. I feel sure that this man will never want all the days of his life since he has become so enthusiastic about his new-found wealth, including the treasures of his subconscious. You possess fabulous and potential wealth in your subconscious mind, unrecognized, unused and unhonored.

How She Learned to Listen to the Voice of Intuition

A few years ago a schoolteacher said to me, "If only I could have known what kind of a man he was, I would not have suffered so much." She had made a mistake in love. She had judged according to appearances and had married a sadist, who almost killed her.

Since then she has listened to the voice of intuition, which means "taught from within." It means the wisdom of your subconscious revealing to you the answer, usually by a predominant hunch, an inner feeling and an awareness that lingers. Intuition is the preceptor of Truth, which transcends the intellect; but we use our reasoning mind to carry out the voice of intuition.

She prays regularly that "Infinite Intelligence reveals to me everything I need to know at all times" and then she follows the lead which comes clearly into her conscious, reasoning mind. She claims constantly that there is nothing hidden that is not made known and that God is her ever present help, guiding her in all her ways. He is a lamp unto her feet and a light upon her path.

Recently she married a wonderful college professor. She said, "The minute I met him I *knew* I would marry him." It was an intuitional perception. They are very happy together. She no longer permits her intellect to reason her away from her intuitional perception.

Your Intuition Is Not Instinct

The tendency of the Cosmic Energizer within you is always to seek to protect you. Its murmurings, whisperings and monitions are always lifeward. A bird builds a nest by instinct, a dog buries a bone and the beaver constructs a dam. These tendencies do not lead to communion with the Divine Presence.

Instinct is simply the self-preservation principle characteristic of all life.

Intuition in man enables him to tune in on the Infinite and bring forth marvelous inventions, discoveries, music, creative ideas and extraordinary and wonderful knowledge not found in books or libraries. It is through intuition that men and women rise to the highest dramatization of artistic genius in music, poetry, painting, science, art, industry and architecture.

A Sales Manager Discovers the Riches of Intuition

It is true that God is an ever present help. A sales manager told me that in hiring employees he found that his first impressions were always correct. His constant prayer is: "Infinite Intelligence reveals to me instantaneously the character and acceptability of every applicant for this concern." He said, "I rarely look at their *résumé*. I follow my intuition, and in over thirty years I have made only one serious mistake. In this case, the man had marvelous references and a friend of mine had recommended him highly. However, he turned out to be as crooked as a ram's horn. He sold some of our research formulas to competing organizations. I did not follow my hunch."

His intuition had been developed by the constant reiteration that Infinite Intelligence reveals to him the right people. His intuition is based on his inner perception of the thoughts and impressions in the subconscious mind of the applicant, enabling him to reject those who would not harmonize with the organization. Intuition is that in man which is called in religious circles his "guardian angel." This sales manager has made a fortune for his organization through his intuitive capacity to select the right men. So can you!

How the Intuitive Voice of the Cosmic Energizer Saved His Mother's Life

While I was conducting a lecture series in Oklahoma City recently a young medical doctor told me that he had started out in his motor car to visit a patient some miles away, when suddenly an inner voice said to him, "Come home. Your mother needs you." The inner voice and feeling that something was wrong persisted with such force that he turned around and drove home as quickly as he could, where he found his mother gasping for breath, apparently from a heart attack. He gave her an injection, put her to bed and in the morning took her to the hospital, where she recovered fully.

He told me that such things happen so often to him that he no longer questions them. A mother and son are always in rapport subconsciously with each other, and, undoubtedly, when she got the attack, she called out for him and he heard, which is clairaudience. He responded and saved her life. His favorite Biblical verse is:—*And the Lord shall guide thee continually* . . . (Isaiah 58:11).

Her Reliance on the Inner Guide Works Wonders for Her

It is now an accepted and well-known truth that the subconscious mind is amenable to control by the conscious mind. According to the law of action and reaction, the conscious mind is reacted upon by the subconscious, which can keep you informed of things transpiring on the subjective plane of life. A policewoman, a detective, told me recently that her constant prayer is, "God is guiding me now and reveals to me everything I need to know instantaneously at all times everywhere."

She said that her first impression is that of the real detective, as she has discovered over the years that the primary feeling she has reflects what is actually taking place in the other person's mentality. What is really in his or her mind is revealed; not what he or she pretends or appears to be. She pointed out that some fellow employees have laughed at her first impressions, but they have discovered through many disappointments that her intuition and first impressions were always right.

In questioning a woman at the police station, for example, she saw inwardly in her mind's eye a bag of cocaine and its location in the woman's home. She and another officer got a search warrant and found it to be exactly where she had seen it clairvoyantly. Her constant impregnation of her subconscious mind that everything she needs to know is revealed to her has conditioned her deeper mind to respond as the answer, the solution, in ways you know not of. The answer could come as clairvoyance, clairaudience, as a hunch, a predominant feeling or sudden flash of an idea in the mind.

She is also a devout Bible student and said to me that she felt that intuition had enabled Joseph to foresee the seven years of famine and had enabled him to protect Egypt against the ravages of starvation. She has cultivated her intuition, and it has brought her honor, respect, promotion and intense inner satisfaction and joy of accomplishment.

RECOGNIZE THE OMNIPRESENCE OF THE COSMIC ENERGIZER

The only reason men and women do not get inspiration and guidance more frequently is because they allow themselves to be distracted by their five senses and the propaganda of the outer world. Intuition leads to a conviction and realization of the Omnipresence of the Infinite One, which is an ever present help in time of trouble.

A SPECIAL PRAYER FOR INTUITION

"The Cosmic Energizer is a lamp unto my feet and a light upon my path. I hear the voice of Truth and I obey it. Through intuition my ears hear and my eyes see all those things which bless, heal and prosper me spiritually and materially. My spiritual intuitions are direct importations of Divine wisdom, and I distinguish clearly between that which is false and that which is true. God reveals to me everything I need to know at all times everywhere. God is an ever present help to me, and I give thanks."

POINTS TO REMEMBER

1. One of the most beautiful prayers in the entire Bible is the 46th Psalm. The first verse says: *God is our refuge and strength; a very present help in trouble.* This simple truth is the finest antidote to fear in the world today.

2. A woman saved herself and companions from a head-on collision by affirming out loud, "God is an ever present

help. God is our refuge." The oncoming motorist suddenly swerved and saved his own life, as well as theirs.

3. An ex-sergeant, whose mother had been praying that he would always be invisible to the enemy and that God would watch over him at all times, found that he actually was invisible to six armed Viet Cong soldiers who shot to death five members of his patrol but paid no attention to him. His mother decreed constantly, "My son will always be invisible to the enemy." His subconscious responded and his life was preserved throughout the campaign.

4. A man, wearing what he called a "good luck piece" given to him by his mother in Greece, was unable to make ends meet during his residence of 35 years in Oklahoma City. At my suggestion he had this talisman, or charm, appraised at a local jeweler's and found it to be worth $30,000. This is a situation experienced by millions of other people. They are unaware of the fabulous treasure-house of potential wealth in their subconscious mind. This man learned to write in his subconscious by repetition and understanding, "God's wealth is circulating in my life and there is always a Divine surplus." Because of his enthusiasm, I feel he will never suffer want during all the days of his life.

5. A woman who had married a sadist now prays regularly that Infinite Intelligence reveals to her everything she needs to know at all times, and she follows the lead which comes clearly into her conscious, reasoning mind. She attracted a wonderful man, a college professor. She said, "The minute I met him I knew he was the one."

This was the inner voice of intuition, revealing to her the answer. She no longer permits her intellect to reason her away from her intuitional perception.

6. Intuition is not instinct. Instinct enables a bird to build a nest according to a pattern bequeathed by the mother bird. For example, when a man first shot birds, the latter transmitted the fears of man to their offspring. Now birds fly away on the approach of the average man. Instinct is self-preservation. Intuition enables man to tune in with the Infinite and bring forth the glories and wonders of the Infinite in science, art, industry, music, poetry and mystic experiences. In other words, intuition enables man to reveal the wisdom of the Infinite and to receive answers to the most profound problems of the ages.

7. A sales manager cultivated his intuitive capacity by constantly reiterating, "Infinite Intelligence reveals to me instantaneously the character and acceptability of every applicant for this concern." In over 30 years he made only one mistake, and that was because he did not follow his "hunch" but listened to the voice of his friend who had recommended an applicant so highly. He looks upon his intuitive capacity as his "guardian angel." He has made a fortune for his organization through his capacity to select the right men.

8. A young medical doctor in Oklahoma City, while motoring to visit a patient, heard the inner voice, "Come home. Your mother needs you." He obeyed the inner voice and arrived in time to give his mother a hypodermic injection for her heart condition, thereby saving her

life. He was in rapport with his mother and, undoubtedly, picked up her thoughts and heard them clearly, which is the faculty of clairaudience. His favorite Biblical verse is:—*And the Lord will guide thee continually . . .* (Isaiah 58:11). These intuitive impulses regarding patients come to him so often he no longer questions them. His subconscious responds to his favorite prayer.

9. A policewoman, a detective, uses a constant prayer, "God is guiding me and reveals to me everything I need to know instantaneously at all times everywhere." Her first impression is the real detective. Her primary impressions prove to be absolutely correct. She has developed clairvoyance and at times sees clearly the contents of the mind of the accused person. In one instance in her mind she saw a bag of cocaine in the drawer in the home of the accused; she got a search warrant and found it to be exactly where she visualized it. She has conditioned her subconscious mind to reveal to her what she needs to know, and it responds in ways we cannot explain.

10. Intuition leads to a conviction and realization of the Omnipresence of the Infinite One, which is an ever present help in time of trouble.

10

How the Cosmic Energizer Can Guide You and Locate Lost Treasures

THERE IS A guiding principle within you, the Cosmic Energizer, which knows only the answer. Recently a woman in Beverly Hills came to me stating that a very valuable diamond ring, which was worth many thousands of dollars was missing. She had looked everywhere for it with no results and thought it might have been stolen.

I suggested that she quiet her mind, relax, let go and talk to the Cosmic Energizer within her as follows: "You are all wise; you know all things; you know where that diamond ring is; you are watching over it, and I know you will reveal to me where it is." She followed this procedure every night prior to sleep, and at the same time, in her imagination, she felt the ring on her finger, the tangibility of it, the naturalness of it, and the solidity of it. She lulled herself to sleep with the words, "Thank you, Father, for my ring."

On the fifth night, she awoke suddenly with the words ringing in her ear, "Look in your car," which she did, and found the ring on the floor of the automobile under the rug. She discovered that there is always an answer when you trust the guiding principle within you.

How the Cosmic Energizer Revealed the Answer and Protected Her from an Operation

A few years ago, during a conference with a young school-teacher, she told me about a recurrent dream, the central episode of which was always the same. Several times a week, when she was sound asleep, a dog would start to bite at her breasts and she would have a terrible struggle, warding the dog off with the bedclothes. On one occasion she fell on the floor, injuring herself badly.

I said to her that undoubtedly her subconscious mind was warning her and that her dream had a special meaning, inasmuch as it had recurred again and again. I suggested she see a medical doctor, which she did. He found two small growths on one of her breasts, both of which his pathologist said were nonmalignant, but that she had come at the right time, as they would have become malignant. These growths were removed, and there has been no return of either one. She was delighted that she had caught the condition in the incipient stage.

The dog biting her breasts in her sleep indicated acute emotional disturbance, and the dog symbolically is a faithful friend. In other words, the guiding principle of her Cosmic Energizer seeks to protect, guide and direct her at all times. She is free from fear, is healthy now, and saturates her mind every day with the 23rd, 27th and 91st Psalms.

HOW THE GUIDING PRINCIPLE SAVED HIM
FROM BANKRUPTCY

Some months ago, in a conference with a businessman operating his own store, he said that he couldn't understand why he was not prospering. His sales were improving, but he was in the red. I suggested that he pray for guidance in the following way: "Infinite Intelligence reveals to me what I need to know about my business, and the answer comes clearly into my conscious, reasoning mind. I follow the lead which comes."

After a few days he felt the urge to ask a special accountant to go over his books, and he found that his trusted bookkeeper, a close relative of his, had been embezzling funds for about two years. He corrected the situation, and now every day he prays that he and his assistants are Divinely guided and that the intelligence of the Infinite governs all their transactions. His regular prayer is that all those working with him are spiritual links in the chain of the organization's growth, welfare and prosperity, and this new attitude has brought about splendid results, financially and in all other respects.

SPIRIT GUIDANCE LEADS TO PRICELESS RELICS

"Fascinating finds of priceless Indian relics, now housed in a museum, are due to spirit guidance," says a Tennessee man in *The National Enquirer*, one of America's largest selling journals.

Kenneth Pennington, a 30-year-old artist, of Rock City Gardens, near Chattanooga, says his ancestors "and their guiding hands" are directing him. His family is descended from Cherokee Indians.

Before each hunt, Pennington offers a ritual and self-composed prayer-song.

"Often I get overwhelming urges to dig in a particular area," he says. "Once, within minutes after singing my prayer, I uncovered the rims of eight beautiful pottery vessels."

Other finds include ornaments, shells, stone tobacco pipes, bones, tools and weapons, some dating from primitive times.

"I'm sure my ancestors know I'm trying to gain scientific knowledge of their past and want to help me," says Pennington.

The museum displays the thousands of rare objects he and his friends were led to find.

At first, his colleagues laughed at his prayers and his "good luck." After Pennington consistently got results. they asked him to sing in the areas where they wanted to dig. His friends' luck also improved.

One night, after finding two skulls several thousand years old, Pennington had a strange dream.

He "saw" one of the skulls with peculiar markings on the forehead.

Next morning when he cleared it, he exposed strange, diamond-shaped markings on the brow. These have never been explained.

Tribute was paid to his finds by E. Raymond Evans, first vice-president of Tennessee Archaeologists Society.

"While many people might doubt the value of Pennington's ritual, his excellent results speak for themselves," says Evans.

The preceding article appeared in *Psychic News*, a newspaper published in London, England, June 2, 1973, issue.

The man mentioned believed that his ancestors were directing him to long lost treasures, and the guiding principle of the Cosmic Energizer responded according to the nature of his request.—*And all things, whatsoever ye shall ask in prayer, believing, ye shall receive* (Matthew 21:22).—*If thou canst believe, all things are possible to him that believeth* (Mark 9:23).

How the Guiding Principle Protected Her

A motion picture actress, who prayed regularly for Divine guidance and right action in her life, had this prodromal dream (a premonitory symptom) every night for about six successive nights in which she was riding a horse up the mountain. The horse would stop several times and struggle to reach the top, but couldn't.

I said to her that a horse is a symbol of emotions, instinct, and its inability to reach the top may indicate some emotional conflict, or impending disease dealing with power and strength. At my suggestion, she consulted a physician, who took a cardiograph and found an impending coronary disorder, which was corrected with rest and nitroglycerin taken as a vasodilator.

Her dream had warned her of an incipient heart attack,

which, by timely action, she prevented. The Cosmic Energizer always seeks to protect, heal and restore the body. Following this experience, she repeats the 100th Psalm every night and the 91st Psalm every morning. For the past six months she has had no symptoms, needs no drugs, and her cardiograph is perfect.

If thou return to the Almighty, thou shalt be built up . . . (Job 22:23). She holds fast to this thought: All healing power comes from God, and is awaiting your recognition.

How the Cosmic Energizer Revealed the Location of a Missing Gold Treasure

An attorney, who is a profound student of the laws of mind, told me of a very interesting way in which the Cosmic Energizer within him revealed a treasure he was seeking. His mother had died suddenly in Canada. She was alone at the time, but neighbors had notified the police and also had phoned him at his home in San Francisco. He flew there and took care of everything, since she had bequeathed everything to him in her will.

He remembered that she had once told him that she had a large collection of foreign gold coins dating back to 1898 and that some day he would inherit them. There was no mention in the will and no trace of them in the house or safe deposit box. At night prior to sleep however, he spoke to his subconscious as follows: "I am now turning this request over to my subconscious mind.* It knows where the gold treasure is and

---

The Power of Your Subconscious Mind by Dr. Joseph Murphy, Prentice-Hall, Inc., Englewood Cliffs, N.J. 1963.

reveals it to me in Divine order, and I recognize the answer."
He lulled himself to sleep with the word, "Answer."

The next morning he felt an overpowering hunch to look
in the attic, and there in an old box covered with magazines
were the coins. Being a numismatist, he knew the value of
the various European gold coins and disposed of them for
over $50,000 in Canadian money.

The Secret of Divine Guidance

Let us suppose you are looking, like this attorney, for lost
treasure or wondering whether to sell your business, buy a certain home, stocks or bonds, dissolve a partnership, move to
London or stay in Los Angeles. Do this: Quiet your mind by
reading, for example, the 23rd Psalm. Remember, it is the
nature of the Cosmic Energizer to respond to your thought.
Action and reaction are universal. The action is your thought
and the reaction is the response from the infinite intelligence
in your deeper mind. Your subconscious is reactive and reflex-
ive; it rebounds, rewards and responds by corresponding to
the nature of your thought patterns. When you contemplate
right action and right results, you will get a reaction from your
deeper mind which represents the guidance you are seeking.

Remember, in seeking guidance, think quietly about right
action. You are using infinite intelligence of your subconscious to the point where it takes over and begins to dominate
you. From there on, your action is controlled by a subjective
wisdom which knows all and sees all. When your thought is
right and your motivation is right, you will be under a subconscious compulsion to do the right thing. Whatever you

impress your subconscious with, good or bad, remember, the law of the subconscious is compulsive.

BE ALERT AND ON THE *QUI VIVE* FOR THE ANSWER

The answer often comes in dreams, visions of the night, hunches, certain symbols, or Biblical verses. If you are a student of the *I Ching*,* the answer can come in a certain hexagram. The ways of your subconscious are past finding out. Mentally devote yourself to the right answer and the response will come. You use the wisdom of your deeper mind to the point where it begins to use you. Practice this technique and you will find that all your ways are pleasant and all your paths are peace.

POINTS TO REMEMBER

1. There is a guiding principle in your subconscious mind which knows all and sees all. A woman lost a very valuable diamond ring and spoke to her subconscious as follows: "You are all wise; you know where the ring is. Reveal to me the answer." This was followed by an overpowering hunch to look in her automobile, where she found it under the rug in the car.

2. Ofttimes guidance comes in a dream or vision of the night. A recurrent dream is very significant. A schoolteacher had a recurrent dream in which a dog was biting her breasts, and she was fighting back with the bedclothes. Actually, her subconscious was warning her of incipient disease. She

---

*See *Secrets of the I Ching* by Dr. Joseph Murphy, Parker Publishing Co., West Nyack, N.Y., 1970.

saw a medical doctor, who found two small growths which he removed, pointing out to her she had come at the right time, as, undoubtedly, had she neglected herself, these would have become malignant. She is free from all fear now, as she meditates regularly on the 23rd, 27th and 91st Psalms.

3. A businessman who was in the red couldn't understand what was wrong. He asked his subconscious mind to reveal to him what he needed to know about his business. An overpowering desire, or hunch, came to him to have a special C.P.A. go over the books, and he found that his bookkeeper, a very close relative, had been embezzling money for over two years. He was saved from bankruptcy and now claims Divine guidance for himself and all his employees. He keeps close tabs on his financial transactions.

4. An Indian gets overwhelming urges to dig in a particular area and discovers ornaments, shells, tools, weapons and other rare objects. He attributes his findings of these long lost treasures to his ancestors' spirit guidance. There is only One Spirit (the Cosmic Energizer), and It responds to all men according to their belief.

5. An actress prayed regularly for Divine guidance and right action in all phases of her life and had a prodromal dream for six successive nights, which depicted her as riding a horse that struggled to reach the top of a mountain but could not. Her subconscious was revealing to her symbolically a heart condition, which her doctor corrected. She nipped an impending coronary attack in the bud and now keeps in perfect health by saturating

her subconscious with the 91st and 100th Psalms every night and morning. The tired horse indicated emotional disturbance, and she followed the lead that came to her. "The Lord (The Cosmic Energizer) makes himself known in a vision and will speak to man in a dream."

6. An attorney found himself at the home of his mother in Canada, who had suddenly passed on. She had told him of a box of ancient gold coins which she possessed and promised to him at her demise. Mention of the gold treasure did not occur in the will, and the coins were nowhere to be found. He turned the request over to his subconscious mind, claiming that the answer would be revealed to him. He was guided by an inner intuition to search in the attic, where he found over $50,000 in gold coins dating back to the early 1890s.

7. The secret of Divine guidance is to think quietly of the Divine solution, knowing there is an infinite intelligence in your subconscious which responds to the nature of your request. When your thought is right and your motivation is right, you will be under a subconscious compulsion to do the right thing. The answers to your requests may come in various ways, such as overpowering hunches, dreams, visions of the night, symbols, Biblical verses or hexagrams of the *I Ching*.* Trust the infinite intelligence to respond and as you have faith and confidence in its response, you will discover the right answer and the day will break for you and all the shadows will flee away.

---

*See *Secrets of the I Ching* by Dr. Joseph Murphy, Parker Publishing Co., Inc., West Nyack, N.Y., 1970.

11

How the Cosmic Energizer Gives You Power of Healing, Power of the Spirit, and Power to Overcome All Obstacles

THE COSMIC ENERGIZER created all of us, as well as the entire world, and the Infinite healing presence indwells all of us. Man did not create himself. He sees a healing presence operating for a period of time after he cuts his finger or burns his hand. This healing presence is in the dog, the cat, and the soil; actually it is omnipresent. Every man and woman can enter into a meaningful relationship with the Cosmic Energizer and thereby heal conditions and solve problems.

WHY SHE WAS NOT DOOMED TO DIE

A few months ago a woman from Nigeria came to see me. She showed me a letter from a relative which stated that she had offended a sorcerer and that he had cursed her and was using the death prayer against her. This woman was on a special assignment here doing some research work.

I explained to her that all this sorcery and voodoo business was purely suggestion and that this sorcerer had no power whatsoever; that the reason she was so perturbed and excited was due to her foolish belief that she was bewitched. Actually, I pointed out to her the suggestion or threat of the sorcerer had no power; it was simply that she accepted it, and it was nothing more than a movement of her own thoughts. She had the power to reject it. She was not in the clutch of a malevolent or a so-called malignant demon; the trouble was fear and terror generated by herself, which attacked all organs in her body.

Accordingly, I told her that this so-called spell could be and would be completely neutralized by following the directions I gave her. I assured her she would be completely free and at peace. I fired her imagination constructively and got her to be receptive to constructive ideas. I gave her a formula to follow three times a day, morning, afternoon and night. She was to affirm: "God is, and His Circle of Love surrounds me. The whole armor of God surrounds me at all times. God's spell of love, peace and harmony envelops me. I bear a charmed life. I am immunized and God intoxicated. I have now received the Divine Antibody and I am free."

We prayed like this together and she went away convinced she would be healed of her fear and superstition. She practiced it faithfully. Gradually all fear left her and she was free. The sequel was very interesting: Her relative wrote asking her what she had done to the sorcerer, as he had died in frightful agony. This young woman no longer received his negative vibrations and they returned with double force to him. Since there was no other place for his evil thoughts to go, his death wish for the other became his own. Fear is the only demon or devil in the world, but faith in God and His Love casts out fear.

In Africa, New Zealand, Australia and other countries where the curse is placed on a victim as one of the local customs, the timely arrival of another "medicine man" or sorcerer using a countercharm restores the victim to perfect health, which indicates that suggestion is at the bottom of the whole thing. One negative, diabolical suggestion given to him, when accepted, kills him (he kills himself due to his abnormal fear), and another suggestion that the spell is removed heals him.

How She Used the Universal Healing Principle

Some months ago I had a letter from a radio lecturer who said, in substance, that he had heard me state that every person in the world has the gift of healing and that certain people are not "chosen" to be healers and endowed with a "particular gift" for the simple reason that God indwells all men and women and that there is only one healing presence lodged in the subconscious of all men.[*] Anyone can set the law of healing into operation, just the same as you can learn to drive an automobile. In order to navigate a plane in the atmosphere, you must study the laws of aerodynamics. In the case of mental and spiritual healing, you must study the laws of mind and the way of the Cosmic Energizer within you.

---

[*]See *The Power of Your Subconscious Mind* by Dr. Joseph Murphy, Prentice-Hall, Inc., Englewood Cliffs, N.J., 1963.

How He Healed Himself

This man who had written the letter said that he was 84 years of age, had had a stroke four years previously, and had been, as he said, out of circulation for that time. His doctor had told him that it was doubtful that he would be able to walk again. His son gave him one of my books, however, *Miracle of Mind Dynamics,** from which he gained the idea of an Infinite Healing Presence, omnipotent and supreme, and he began to claim boldly, many times a day, that this power was healing him now and that God walks and talks in him. His son heard him frequently giving thanks for his miraculous healing. At the same time he imagined himself on the golf course, feeling the grip of the iron, the touch of the golf ball, and hearing the conversation of his friends and the congratulations of his son. He imagined all this with deep sensory vividness until his mental picture had all the tones of reality.

At the end of two months he was back on the golf course and is still walking. This man's faith and disciplined imagination resurrected the powers of the Infinite, to which all things are possible. God can do for us only that which he does through us.

STEPS TO PRACTICE IN THE HEALING PROCESS

1. Turn away from the ugly picture; when you choose to acknowledge the Infinite Healing Power, this is an act

---

*Miracle of Mind Dynamics by Dr. Joseph Murphy, Prentice-Hall, Inc., Englewood Cliffs, N.J., 1964.

of faith, because you are recognizing the only Presence, Power, Cause and Substance.

2. Contemplate God from the highest standpoint and claim that Divine Love and harmony saturate your whole being.

3. Quietly decree that the Infinite Healing Presence—The Great Physician—is silently and constantly permeating every atom of your being, reproducing wholeness, beauty and perfection where the imperfection is.

4. As you follow this procedure there is a perfect response taking place subconsciously. Continue to give thanks for the action of the Healing Presence, and wonders will happen as you pray this way.

THE WONDERS OF THE COSMIC ENERGIZER

This is the Power and the Energy that guides the planets and the stars in their courses. This is the same Power that governs the billions of cells in your body. This Infinite Power and Healing Presence is seeking an outlet through you. Trust It; believe in It. Realize that your body is basically spiritual substances, not just flesh and blood. Let this Power flow through you. Do not hinder It by fear and doubt.

The Cosmic Energizer is Omnipotent. It is far greater than all the power generated by atomic or nuclear energy, or that of the laser beam, or even that of all the motors in the world, or all the planes flying the skies of the world. Contemplate this Cosmic Energizer that hurls this planet through space while guiding the billions and billions of stars and suns in their courses in the galaxies of space. Surrender to this Power and let It flow through your body, finances, business, home life, and all phases of your life. Let wonders happen in your life.

The Wonderful Power of the Spirit

The Bible says:—*God is a Spirit . . .* (John 4:24). Spirit is that which is invisible and eternal; it cannot deteriorate, can't grow old or become exhausted. It is timeless, ageless and formless. You are Spirit. Your body is, of course, spiritual also. Spirit was never born and cannot die. Spirit is the Reality of you. You are unchanging Spirit in your true nature. The world we see about us is Spirit in manifestation.

How He Realized the Power of the Spirit

The late Dr. Harry Gaze, who was an international lecturer on the psychology of daily living, told me that at one time in London he had great difficulty speaking, and a Harley Street specialist told him there was a growth in his lung that needed to be excised. He thanked the doctor and told him he would call back in a few days' time for another appointment.

That evening in his hotel he dwelt on the aspect of God, or Spirit, unchanging, eternal, absolutely whole, perfect, timeless, changeless and ageless. He began to realize that his lungs were spiritual ideas created by God and that his lungs were spiritual substance. As he continued to pray for over an hour that his lungs were spiritual ideas functioning perfectly, there was a slight hemorrhage during the night and in the morning he went to the specialist. The latter said, "Your lungs are perfect. What happened?" Dr. Gaze told him how he had prayed, and he said that the specialist wrote it down word for word and was deeply impressed. This doctor realized that matter is Spirit in form.

LEARNING TO COMMUNE WITH THE SPIRIT WITHIN

St. Augustine said: "Thou hast made us for Thyself and our hearts are restless until we find our rest in Thee." The Psalmist said: *As the hart panteth after the water brooks, so panteth my soul after thee, O god* (Psalm 42:1).

Every man hungers for union with the Source of his being. This hunger can be satisfied by realizing that his own growth is the unfolding of all the qualities, powers and aspects of the Spirit within him, in the same manner as a tree grows from a pattern and life forces which are within the seed. The oak, for example, is already in the acorn.

God, or Spirit, is involved in man, and man is here to evolve, portray and reveal the powers of the Infinite Spirit within him. There are mental and spiritual laws as well as so-called physical ones. Anyone can learn how to use his mental and spiritual powers resident within him. For example, the laws of your subconscious mind are as dependable as the laws of electronics or chemistry, and they have equally predictable results.

You can learn to dissolve poverty, sickness, prejudice, fear and limitations of all kinds in your life by cooperating with the laws of Mind and Spirit. Infinite Spirit (the Cosmic Energizer) is not to blame for sickness, lack and limitation; it is due to our wrong thinking, which may be due to ignorance, apathy or wrong choice on our part which creates our own so-called hell here on earth.

How Spirit of Forgiveness Solved Her Problem

A young woman employed by the Government claimed she had been undermined by an associate, who deliberately lied to her superiors about her and that, as a consequence, she was demoted to an inferior position with less pay and prestige. She suffered from chronic ulcers because of her ulcerated thoughts.

At my suggestion she decided to forgive herself as well as the other girl. To forgive means to give forth love, goodwill, harmony and all the blessings of life on all people everywhere. This is absolutely essential for spiritual, mental and physical well being. I explained to this young lady that as long as she held on to resentment, hostility, the condemnation of others or of herself, the memory of an injury, hurt, or failure, brooding over the past, recalling old grudges and old wrongs, she would create stoppage and congestion. By her attitude she was obstructing the flow of Infinite Life and love. She should realize that yesterday ended last night.

She decided to heal herself, and, realizing she had been hurting herself by her negative, destructive thoughts, she came to a decision as follows: "I release ____ to Infinite Spirit and I wish for her health, happiness and peace. Whenever I think of her, I will affirm: 'I released you. God be with you.'" She also forgave herself and resolved not to think resentful or hateful thoughts any more.

She discovered after three or four days she could meet the other woman in her mind and she was at peace. Her ulcers disappeared in about ten days.—*And shall put my spirit in you, and ye shall live . . .* (Ezekiel 37:14).

HOW THE COSMIC ENERGIZER OVERCAME
HIS GREAT OBSTACLES

Imagination is called the eye of the soul. Truly, the world of imagination is boundless. As Shakespeare says, ". . . gives to airy nothing a local habitation and a name."

A few months ago an officer who had returned from Vietnam came to see me and told me that he had made some poor investments on the stock market and was broke. He added that he had accumulated debts, his wife was in the county hospital as he had no funds to send her to a private hospital, and he was about to lose his home. He looked at all these obstacles as insuperable barriers.

I spent some time with him teaching him the laws of mind and gave him one of my very popular books, *Your Infinite Power to be Rich*,* suggesting that he read Chapter 11, Mental Imagery and Riches. In about a week's time he returned full of enthusiasm and bubbling over with energy and vitality.

This is what he told me: "I read and reread Chapter 11, and I said to myself, 'If mental imagery can create riches for others, it can do it for me.' An old army friend of mine who was concerned about me invited me to the race track in order to take my mind off my problems. The night before I went, I studied the races and began to imagine I was going seven times to the window collecting a large sum of money each time. My friend had loaned me one hundred dollars, saying, 'You know horses. You'll win a fortune tomorrow.' I imagined

---

Your Infinite Power to Be Rich by Dr. Joseph Murphy, Parker Publishing Co., Inc., West Nyack, N.Y., 1966.

going to each window over and over again until I felt the reality of it all. Each time in my vivid imagination I imagined the cashier giving me a large sum of money.

"I did this for about three hours and finally fell asleep. Then, the most amazing thing happened. I dreamed the seven winners in the seven races and gave my friend the seven winning names. He bet large sums of money on each, informing me that if they won I would receive 50 percent. I personally won about $2000 and he won $35,000. He gave me $17,500, which solved my present problems, and now I have a wonderful position with a starting salary of $25,000."

This man created an imaginary drama, and through frequent habitation of his mind he felt the naturalness of it all. He repeated the scene over and over in his imagination until it jelled in his subconscious mind.

—*Call unto me, and I will answer thee, and shew thee great and mighty things, which thou knowest not* (Jeremiah 33:3).

How the Cosmic Energizer Makes Your Dream Come True

People laughed openly at Charles B. Darrow, a down-and-out salesman who spent most of his time dreaming about what he would do if only he could get control of a few railroads . . . or a string of hotels . . . or a bank or two.

They laughed even harder when the 40-year-old Darrow made himself a stack of play money and began pretending he was a millionaire making big financial deals.

But the ridicule didn't seem to bother Darrow. He told everyone: "Never dream a little dream."

Darrow lost his job in 1929 and during the Great Depression he kept the wolf from his door by doing odd jobs. Things got so bad in 1930 that he couldn't even pay his rent at times. But he kept thinking of high finance and big real estate deals.

"With my play money and an imaginary financial empire laid out on a piece of linoleum, I killed time by juggling mythical investments." Darrow recalled years later. Friends and neighbors who went to Darrow's Germantown, Pa., home to hoot at him found themselves strangely interested in his fantasy world of high finance.

"First thing you knew we'd all be sitting down and competing excitedly for high stakes—in play money, of course," he said.

Then a thought struck him. If his make-believe financial empire interested his friends so much, it might interest others too.

Unable to think small, he made up some sets of the game and took them to no less an outlet than Wanamaker's, the prestigious department store in Philadelphia. They sold.

"Then, without spending a nickel on advertising, I began getting calls for more sets, and more still, until I could not make them all in my basement."

That was the end of the Depression for Charles B. Darrow. He became rich, retiring on a 37-acre estate in Bucks County, Pa., where he lived until his death at 78 in 1967.

For Darrow, when he was dead broke but dreaming big dreams, had invented the greatest high-finance game of all time—Monopoly.

The preceding article by Joseph Cassidy appeared in *The National Enquirer*, September 16, 1973. Dream lofty dreams, and as you dream so shall you become. But be sure to put the foundation of faith and confidence in the Power of God to bring it to pass.

POINTS TO REMEMBER

1. The Infinite Healing Presence indwells all of us, including the animal world and the soil we walk on. It is omnipresent. Man did not create himself, and it is reasonable to assume that the Cosmic Energizer which did create him can heal and restore him.

2. A woman from Nigeria believed that a curse was pronounced upon her by a voodoo sorcerer in her native land. She became terribly agitated, emotionally disturbed and mentally ill. It was explained to her that the suggestions of others have no power except we give them power, and that it was a movement of her own thoughts that caused her turbulence. She was doing research work in Los Angeles and was highly educated, but was a victim of the primitive beliefs in the power of witchcraft and maledictions pronounced by witch doctors. She learned the laws of her mind. She completely rejected the suggestion and affirmed that God's love surrounded her and that one with God was a majority.

She saw that there was nothing to oppose Omnipotence, while at the same time she poured out God's blessings on the voodoo witch doctor. She was free of fear, and was surprised to discover that he had died suddenly in great pain. He had actually killed himself. He suffered from the proverbial boomerang. The negative force he hurled came back to him with double strength and killed him.

3. Anyone can set the law of healing into operation by learning the laws of mind, in the same way for example, as you learn to drive your car. The Infinite Healing Presence responds to your thoughts and to your beliefs.

4. A man aged 84, who had had a stroke, began to claim boldly many times a day that the miraculous Healing Power of God was now healing him; at the same time he gave thanks constantly for the healing that was taking place. Though ill, he constantly imagined himself on the golf course with all the sensory vividness at his command and within two months he found himself on the golf course, perfectly whole, vital and strong.

5. Steps in healing are as follows: Turn away from the problem or conditions. Contemplate the Infinite Healing Presence saturating your whole being, vitalizing, healing and restoring you, and continue to give thanks for the healing which is taking place every moment of the day, and wonders will happen as you pray.

6. The Cosmic Energizer is the Power that moves the world, governs the galaxies in space and hurls the planets through space. This Power is greater than all the energy generated by atomic bombs, nuclear fission and

laser beams. Surrender to this Power and let Its benefi-
cent healing balm flow through your body, business,
home life and finances.

7. God is Spirit, and Spirit is invisible, timeless, changeless
and ageless. It was never born and will never die. Water
wets It not; fire burns It not; wind blows It not away;
swords pierce It not. Spirit is the Reality of you—this is
why you are immortal. Dr. Harry Gaze, world lecturer,
had a growth in his lung and began to contemplate that
Spirit, or God, was the reality of him and that his lungs
were spiritual substance. He began to realize that Spirit
was whole, perfect, unchanging and eternal. He affirmed
for an hour slowly, quietly and with deep understanding
that his lungs were spiritual ideas in the mind of God
and that they were functioning perfectly. At night he
experienced a slight hemorrhage in his lungs, but in the
morning the doctor found his lungs perfect. Dr. Gaze,
in contemplating the Divine ideal, had brought about a
molecular change to conform to the perfect idea held in
the mind of God.

8. Man is basically a religious being. St. Augustine said:
"Thou hast made us for Thyself and our hearts are restless until they find repose in thee." God, or Infinite
Spirit, is involved in man and man is here to evolve and
bring forth all the qualities, attributes and potencies of
Infinite Spirit. The laws of your subconscious mind are
just as dependable as the laws of chemistry or electronics. Any idea felt as true is impressed on your subconscious and comes forth on the screen of space as form,
function, experience or event. This is why man can make

his own heaven—harmony and peace—or his own hell—misery and suffering.

9. To forgive means to give forth love, goodwill, harmony and all the blessings of life on all people. You know when you have forgiven others, because you can meet them in your mind and there is no longer any sting. Holding onto grudges, resentments and old hurts creates stoppage and congestion.

10. The Cosmic Energizer can overcome the greatest obstacle in your life, whether sickness, financial problems or barriers of any kind. A retired Army officer was completely broke, about to lose his home, unable to take care of his wife, and obligated for a number of debts which he was unable to meet. He read one of my books, *Infinite Power to Be Rich*, and became fascinated with the chapter on Mental Imagery and Riches. A friend invited him to the races, and the night before his visit to the race track, he imagined over and over again that he was going seven times to the window, collecting large sums of money. He did this for about three hours and fell asleep. In a dream he identified the winners of seven consecutive races, woke up and wrote the names down. He gave the names to his friend, who made $35,000 and gave him one-half of the winnings. He made $2000 himself. This solved his problem, gave him new courage, and he found a position paying $25,000 a year to start.

11. Charles Darrow was broke in 1929. He began to imagine, however, that he had lots of money and land. He began to play with play money, creating an imaginary financial empire and making mythical investments. He

laid the game out on linoleum. Friends became interested in his game, and participated with him in competing excitedly for high stakes in play money. He accumulated millions in real money and a vast estate by dreaming up the high-finance game of all time—Monopoly. He put a foundation under his dream. He knew that whatever he imagined and felt to be true would come to pass.

12

How the Cosmic Energizer Can Breathe the Breath of Life

THIS BOOK DEALS with the Cosmic Energizer, which is God in action. God is the Living Spirit Almighty within all men. Many scientists use the term Energy instead of Spirit (God). The word energy comes from the Greek *energeia*: en, "in"; ergon, "work." There is only One Supreme Energy or Power, and all the energies in the world are simply modifications of that One Cosmic Energizer.

All kinds of energy are ultimately measured in terms of work. As a matter of fact, energy may also be defined as your capacity to do work. Energy may become manifest in many ways; or, to put it another way, there are many forms of energy. In this book we are not primarily concerned with mechanical energy, but rather with man's capacity to energize and vitalize his thoughts, images, dreams and the inspirations of his heart and bring them to pass on the screen of space.

Einstein and other scientists have pointed out the inter-convertibility and interchangeability of energy and matter, which illustrates the truth of the ancient Vedas, wherein it states that matter is the lowest degree of Spirit and Spirit is the highest degree of matter. In other words, matter is Energy or Spirit in form.

This universe is the house of the Eternal Light or Life, the Energy which we call God. This One Energizer is your Awareness, the I AM or Life Principle, which is the actor in your body and also in the universe. For the purpose of manifestation the One Energy divided Itself into two (the masculine principle and the feminine principle). These two are sometimes referred to as the superior and inferior natures, or the conscious and subconscious mind. Your conscious mind conveys ideas and images to your subconscious mind, and the latter determines how your thoughts and images become manifest as form, function and experience in your life.

WHAT THIS COSMIC ENERGY CAN DO FOR YOU

This intensely real force can guide you and open up new doors of expression for you. It can liberate you from the midst of failure, sickness, lack and limitation. Moreover, this invisible intelligence can solve your problems, banish your difficulties and set you on the royal road to riches, freedom, joy and new opportunities to express yourself at higher levels. This Cosmic Energizer can illumine your pathway and enable you to mold, fashion and direct your own destiny. It has the magical power to bring peace to the troubled mind and the healing love of the Infinite to the broken heart.

This Cosmic Energizer, which is God in you, can inspire you and reveal to you everything you need to know; all you have to do is to open your mind and your heart to receive. Let this Divine Energy reveal to you your true place in life and also open up the way for your fulfillment. It can attract to you the right partner, associate, or spouse possessing kindred spirits, who harmonizes with you in all ways. Furthermore, you can experience prosperity and success beyond your fondest dreams.

How Cosmic Energy Restored Her Soul to Peace

Some time ago I talked to a woman who had suffered with colitis for over a year. Sedation and diet alleviated the distress and pain to some degree, but she had lost considerable weight and she had found it necessary to buy a new wardrobe. I told her that according to research work done by psychosomatic doctors, colitis was usually due to deep-seated resentment, hostility and suppressed rage. She then admitted that her mother-in-law was the anchor that bound her to the wheel of pain.

Her Plan of Forgiveness

She came to a clear-cut decision and affirmed with faith and confidence: "I forgive myself for harboring negative thoughts and destructive thoughts about my mother-in-law and resolve not to do this any more. Any time I think of her, I will immediately put some spiritual iodine on my thought and affirm, 'I release you to God, and I wish for you all the blessings of life.'"

In a few weeks' time she had the customary examination

and was found to be completely normal. She had used Cosmic Energy constructively.

—*He restoreth my soul* . . . (Psalm 23:3).

Let Cosmic Energy Fulfill Your Goals in Life

If you have an unfulfilled desire, dream or goal, you may be harboring in your mind some thoughts of fears or worry, or you may be seeing barriers to its fulfillment. Identify yourself now with your goal by mentally and emotionally uniting with it. Energize your ideal in your mind by frequently visioning its fulfillment. As you add one brick to another in the building of your house, your sustained energy will gradually grow and magnify until your subconscious mind is full of the quality of your thought and feeling. As you persevere and remain faithful to your vision, Cosmic Energy will flow through your mental pattern and cause your desire to cross over from the conscious sphere of life to the subjective state of awareness, or subconscious embodiment.

God the Cosmic Energizer

A banker friend of mine said to me, "I prefer the term Cosmic Energizer to that of God. I know they mean the same thing. I know, of course, that God, which is Universal Energy, created the cosmos and initiated the entire evolutionary process and started the universe on its inexorable path, which knows no end."

HOW HE RECHARGES HIS MENTAL
AND SPIRITUAL BATTERIES

Every morning this banker sets aside five or ten minutes in his den, quiets his mind and boldly claims: "The invigorating, rejuvenating Cosmic Energizer is now active in me, filling my whole being with energy, vitality, youth, vigor and strength. Every moment of the day I am growing stronger, healthier, happier and more vital. My mental and spiritual batteries are now recharged by the vitalizing power of the Cosmic Energizer."

This banker is bubbling over with enthusiasm and is moving onward, upward and Godward.

HOW HE RECEIVES WONDERFUL ANSWERS

A young scientist working in the space industry told me how he had fished many wonderful ideas out of the depths of his subconscious mind. He quiets his mind and thinks about the desired answer, knowing the Cosmic Energy will flow through in response to his thought. He listens quietly for any bit of guidance that comes, joining all the threads together. Ofttimes the whole answer comes like a graph in his conscious mind. He is aware that the Cosmic Energizer knows only the answer.

Remember, your conscious mind, when it is still, receives wisdom, guidance and answers to problems from your Deeper mind. When you cannot solve your problem with your conscious mind, become a good executive and turn the request over with confidence to your subconscious, thereby energizing the subjective forces, resulting in an answer.

Setting the Cosmic Energizer to Work for You

Get as clear an idea as possible of what you wish to know or have answered. Dwell upon the answer from many angles. Try to solve it with your conscious, reasoning mind, giving it a high degree of attention, and you will thereby energize the wisdom of your subconscious mind. As you go to sleep at night, you could say to your subconscious: "Give your attention to this and reveal to me the answer." You may do this silently or audibly, whichever appeals to you. When you awaken in the morning, the answer may be on your lips. If not, realize you have turned your request over with faith and confidence, and the answer will come in Divine order. It may come as a sudden flash to your conscious mind just exactly when you need the answer or data.

The Cosmic Energizer Gives Him Amazing Answers

Recently, at the request of Dr. William Parker, author of *Your Prayer Can Change Your Life*,* I spoke in Anaheim to members of the Spiritual Frontiers Foundation, and one of the men attending the meeting talked with me prior to the session, stating that all his life he had been intensely interested in racing and now goes all over the country to the most prominent race tracks. He said that he studies one important race prior to sleep, checking up on past performances of each horse; then he mentions each horse by name and says to his subconscious, "Give me the Number One winner." He added that It always does.

---

*Published by Prentice-Hall, Inc., Englewood Cliffs, N.J.

Apparently he lives well and has all the money he needs to achieve whatever he wants to do, when he wants to do it. He reasons that when he asks his subconscious to awaken him at a certain hour, it does so; also, when he commands it feelingly and knowingly to remind him of an appointment, it does exactly that. From that premise, he proceeded to make a small fortune and a wonderful livelihood by studying horses from all angles and then concentrating on the winner in the most important race the day before the races. The answer always comes to him in a vivid dream. Due to his discipline, study and fascination for horses, he activates the Cosmic Energizer in his subconscious mind, with the result that he dreams the outcome of the particular race on which he has focused his thoughts.

This man fills his mind with all the information on the horses in the race, consulting "dope sheets" and past performances, and then concentrates exclusively on the winner prior to sleep. This is etched in his subconscious mind, where it gestates in the darkness; then the subconscious presents it full-blown into his conscious mind.

HE LEARNED HIS COSMIC ENERGIZER KNOWS
ONLY THE ANSWER

During a conversation with a businessman some weeks ago, he told me how he got the money to go into partnership with another man. He had read *The Power of Your Subconscious Mind*,* and one night he said to his subconscious prior to

---

The Power of Your Subconscious Mind by Dr. Joseph Murphy, Prentice-Hall, Inc., Englewood Cliffs, N.J., 1963.

sleep, "You are all-wise. You know the answer to everything. I am interested in two gold stocks, Campbell Red Lake and Homestake. Reveal to me which one I should buy for a quick profit." He relaxed, let go completely, and dropped off to the deep of sleep. In a dream a man appeared opening a can of Campbell soup and offered him some. He awakened and knew immediately that the symbol meant Campbell Red Lake.

He bought several thousand shares, and in a short period of time it went up 40 points, netting him a profit of over $80,000, which enabled him to pay $60,000 for a one-half interest in a thriving business. This man knew intuitively that gold shares were about to rise and actually go through the roof, as he explained it, and he summoned the Cosmic Energizer, requesting the answer, secure in the conviction that the answer would be revealed to him.

THE WONDER-WORKING POWER OF THE COSMIC ENERGIZER

When you cut yourself, the wisdom of your Cosmic Energizer activates the phagocytes, which kill any septic germs that might infect the wound. Furthermore, it coagulates the blood, heals the cut, and weaves the new skin. It also controls all the vital organs of your body such as your breathing, digestion, circulation and all phases of your life.

Herbert Spencer says: "Amid all the mysteries by which we are surrounded, nothing is more certain than that we are ever in the presence of an Infinite and Eternal Energy from which all things proceed." Man is waking up to the fact that God indwells man rather than operating or influencing man from without. Your thought is energy and has a rate of vibration. If you think of the Cosmic Energizer, or God, your thought has the highest rate of vibrations and it neutralizes and destroys thoughts of fear, lack, doubt, etc., in the same manner as that in which the sun dissolves the mist or the light casts out darkness.

Ralph Waldo Emerson said: "There is no thought in my mind but it quickly tends to convert itself into a power and organizes a huge instrumentality of means."

—*As he thinketh in his heart, so is he* . . . (Proverbs 23:7).

POINTS TO REMEMBER

1. The Cosmic Energizer is God in action in our lives. Scientists use the term *Energy* for God, which is the Living Spirit Almighty animating all things. All energies in the world—mechanical, electrical or atomic—are simply modifications of the One Universal Cosmic Energy.

2. Man can energize and give life to his dreams, his ideals and the aspirations of his heart and bring them to pass on the screen of space.

3. For the purpose of creation, the Cosmic Energizer divided Itself into two principles, one masculine the other feminine. In everyday, psychological language, those two phases represent your conscious and subconscious mind.

4. The Cosmic Energizer within you can guide you and open up new doors of expression for you. It can liberate you from the midst of failure, sickness, lack and limitation. Moreover, this invisible intelligence can solve your

problems, banish your difficulties and prosper you beyond your fondest dreams.

5. This Cosmic Energizer can illumine your pathway and enable you to mold, fashion and shape your own destiny. It can bring peace to the troubled mind and reveal to you everything you need to know at all times everywhere.

6. A woman with colitis, who was full of resentment, decided to forgive herself for harboring destructive thoughts, and she began to radiate love and goodwill toward her mother-in-law until her mind came to a state of peace. She released the healing power of the Cosmic Energizer and was made completely whole.

7. Identify yourself with your goal or desire by mentally and emotionally uniting with it. As you do this, the Cosmic Energizer will activate the power of your subconscious mind and bring it to pass.

8. A banker recharges his mental and spiritual batteries this way: Every morning he sets aside five minutes or more and claims that the invigorating, rejuvenating Cosmic Energizer is now active in him, filling his whole being with energy, vitality and youth. He is a transformed man, full of vitality, zest, enthusiasm and the elan of life.

9. A space scientist receives wonderful answers by quieting his mind and thinking of the answer he desires, while knowing that the Cosmic Energizer will flow through his thought as the answer. He listens quietly for every bit of guidance that comes, weaving all the threads together, and lo and behold, the answer appears full-blown in his mind.

10. As you go to sleep at night, say to your subconscious, "Give your attention to this and reveal to me the answer." Do this silently or audibly. Ofttimes when you awaken in the morning, the first thought you have is the answer. It may also come in a dream or vision of the night; or, when preoccupied with something else, the idea or solution flashes spontaneously into your conscious mind.

11. A race horse enthusiast informed me that the way he makes a fabulous income is by studying thoroughly the backgrounds of all the horses in a particularly important race. Having gathered all the information possible, he focuses all his attention on that one particular race and speaks to his subconscious, saying: "Give me the Number One winner." He lulls himself to sleep with that one idea. His subconscious responds in a vivid dream, showing him clearly the winner, and he bets accordingly. His attitude is:—*If thou canst believe, all things are possible to him that believeth* (Mark 9:23).

12. A businessman received wonderful information on two gold stocks, Homestake and Campbell Red Lake. He spoke to his subconscious as follows: "You are all-wise. You know the answer. Reveal which of these stocks I should buy for a quick profit." In a dream a man appeared opening a can of Campbell soup, and he immediately knew that this was the symbolic answer. His investment increased about 40 points in a short period of time, making him an $80,000 profit.

13. The Cosmic Energizer, which is the Infinite Healing Presence within you, governs all your vital organs; transmutes

the food you eat to tissue, muscle, blood and bone; releases a defense mechanism in case of infection; and seeks to preserve you and watch over you at all times.

14. Your thought is energy, and when your thoughts are God's thoughts, God's power is with your thoughts of good.

13

How the Cosmic Energizer Can Increase the Joys of Marriage

MANY PEOPLE ENTER into marriage without praying for guidance or Divine right action. Marriage, to be real, must first be on a spiritual basis. There must be a union of two hearts. Some women say that they want to get married for security, or that they want a home. Such an attitude is wrong. Security comes from being in tune with the Cosmic Energizer, which releases more and more creative ideas, harmony, peace, protection and guidance along all lines.

When men marry because the girl is very pretty or because she has a lot of money or political influence, they embark on partnerships which have the wrong foundation. This is wrong because they are not founded on love, which is a movement of the heart. The mere fact that they are married in a church does not necessarily sanctify the marriage or make it real.

THE COSMIC ENERGIZER AND THE LAW OF ATTRACTION

We attract others according to our mental and spiritual wavelengths; in other words, like attracts like. Our mental attitude determines our experience. We must establish the mental equivalent of that which we want in life. We do this by quietly thinking with interest on the ideal we wish to accomplish, and gradually we succeed in establishing the mental equivalent in our mind.

THE IDEAL WAY TO ATTRACT THE RIGHT MAN INTO YOUR LIFE

If a woman uses the following prayer night and morning, knowing that like a seed deposited in the ground which grows after its kind, likewise will the qualities and characteristics of the man on whom she meditates come forth into her experience in the form of the ideal husband:

"Infinite Intelligence attracts to me a man who is marriageable and who has a reverence for the Divinity which shapes our ends. He is spiritual, loyal, faithful, talented, prosperous and successful in life. He harmonizes with me perfectly, spiritually, mentally and physically. He loves my ideals and I love his ideals. He does not want to make me over, and I don't want to make him over. There are mutual love, freedom and respect between us. He comes without encumbrances. It is an act of providence and makes all things new. The intelligence of the Cosmic Energizer within me brings both of us together in Divine order."

Be sure you do not subsequently deny what you are affirming, because you would then neutralize the prayer process. It would be like pressing up and down at the same time in an elevator.

CONTEMPLATE WHAT YOU HAVE TO OFFER A MAN

Dwell on your good points, while realizing you are honest, sincere, loving and kind. You appreciate a lovely home. You have the amenities of life. You can entertain. You can cherish, love and admire the man, and be a tremendous asset to him. Think of all the wonderful qualities you have and let that be your mental broadcast. You are not a nagger, abnormally jealous, a gambler or an alcoholic. On the contrary, you have so much love, peace and kindness to give that by the law of reciprocal relationship, you will attract a man who will love, cherish and admire you also.

If you are a man seeking a wife, ask yourself first what you have to give a wife. Dwell on your good points such as: You are honest, sincere, faithful, loyal, have a very good income and are in a position to furnish an ideal place in which to live. You also realize that if you love a woman, you do not do or say anything unloving, since you want to see her happy, joyous and fully expressed.

THE RIGHT SPIRITUAL APPROACH TO
ATTRACTING THE IDEAL WIFE

Pray quietly and with interest, using the following prayer: "Infinite Intelligence attracts to me the ideal woman, who is marriageable. She is graceful, charming, honest, sincere, loyal, and has a deep reverence for the great eternal truths of God. There are mutual love, freedom and respect between us. I am mentally and spiritually united to these qualities of the woman I want, and I know that as I meditate on these qualities they will sink down by osmosis to my subconscious mind and I will attract a woman who will be the embodiment of my ideal in Divine order through Divine love."

Affirm these truths quietly and with interest night and morning, and when they are subjectified you will automatically attract the right woman and there will be mutual love and understanding. When a seed is placed in the ground, it dies first and then bequeaths its energy to another form of itself. Likewise, the qualities of the ideal woman you are dwelling on will become subjectified and then the deeper currents of your mind will bring both of you together in Divine order.

How to Experience True Marriage

Marriage is an accord of Divine ideals, a harmony and a purity of purpose. Harmony, honesty, love and integrity must prevail in the minds and hearts of both husband and wife. Marriage is a union of two souls united by love and respect for each other. When there is a true, spiritual union between two people, there is no divorce, for none is wanted. They blend spiritually, mentally and physically. This is the meaning of:—*What therefore God hath joined together, let not man put asunder* (Matthew 19:6).

How the Cosmic Energizer Can Bring Love and Companionship in Your Golden Years

The author has performed many marriage ceremonies for men and women of 70, 80 and 90 years, chronologically speaking. Many men have stated that they are impotent sexually; nevertheless, God (love) joined them together with the women of their choice for the simple reason that they were honest, sincere and just with each other. In other words, there was perfect understanding between the man and the woman. Honesty, truth, justice and sincerity and children of love; therefore, these marriages were entered into reverently, thoughtfully and with a deep understanding of its spiritual significance. They sought a loving companionship in which they desired to share their joys and experiences together. Their marriages were true unions of two souls seeking their way back to the heart of Reality.

She Asked, "Should I Get a Divorce?"

This is an individual matter and cannot be generalized. Divorce may be right in some cases and wrong in others. Anyone can tell you to go and get a divorce, but ofttimes that is not the solution any more than is marriage the solution for a lonely person. A divorced woman may be far more honest, noble and sincere than many of her married friends who are living a lie rather than facing the truth.

Many engage in various alibis and excuses such as: It would be bad for political, religious or business reasons. Others say they don't get a divorce because of the children or any number of other rationales. It is far better to have the child live with one parent or relative who really loves him than to be brought up under the influence of a father and mother who quarrel, argue and are full of hostility to one another. Children grow up in the image and likeness of the dominant mental and emotional climate of the home.

When a Marriage Is Not a Marriage

Some time ago I had a conference with a woman who had been married in San Francisco. She had known the man she married for about six months. He took her to the most expensive restaurants and shows in the city and gave her expensive presents. He had told her that he was a private investigator, but she later discovered cocaine, marijuana, and other drugs in his traveling bags. When she confronted him with the evidence, he admitted he was trafficking in dope and going to Mexico frequently for his pickups. This was no marriage for the simple reason that he had lied to her. She had been deceived and tricked.

At my suggestion she conferred with an attorney and brought about the dissolution of the marriage. She was wealthy and had political connections which, as her husband admitted, was the real reason he had married her. Such a marriage is nothing more than a sham, a farce and a masquerade.

How She Increased the Joy in Marriage

A divorced man who had married a woman of another religious persuasion felt guilty and feared that he would be punished, because in his eyes he had sinned. He was confused

because of his misinterpretation of the Biblical quotation,—
*Whosoever shall put away his wife, except it be for fornication,
and shall marry another, committeth adultery: and whoso marrieth
her which is put away doth commit adultery* (Matthew 19:9).
The Bible also says:—*Whosoever looketh on a woman to lust
after her hath committed adultery with her already in his heart*
(Matthew 5:28).

The explanation to this man was the cure and the freedom
from a guilt complex. We are told that adultery is of the
heart, and that the latter is the old name for the subconscious
mind. The heart is the seat of the emotions, the feeling
nature, the subjective side of man. Acts of the body are determined by the movement of the mind. I explained to this
man that men and women mentioned in the Bible represent
the interaction of the conscious and subconscious mind. The
conscious mind in the Bible is called the husband and the
subconscious is referred to as the wife.

Adultery in the Bible is an old English word meaning idolatry, i.e., giving allegiance and attention to false gods rather
than the one true God—The Cosmic Energizer—which is
supreme and sovereign. The Bible is a mental and spiritual
textbook, and it points out that when man visits the slums in
his own mind and cohabits with evil in the bed of his mind,
he is really committing fornication and adultery, Biblically
speaking. A man who condemns himself and indulges in
hate, resentment, anger or ill will is definitely cohabiting with
evil and is, therefore, guilty of fornication and adultery. He is
already divorced because he has mentally separated himself
from his marriage vows and is no longer married or emotionally attached to peace, harmony, love and understanding.

He learned also that the Life Principle, or Cosmic Energizer, never condemns or punishes. We do this to ourselves by the way we think and feel. Marriage rules and regulations vary among the different states and countries. All these were created by ecclesiastical bodies of various beliefs. Love knows no creed, dogma, race or nationality. Love transcends all those things. God is impersonal and is no respecter of persons.

This man decided to forgive himself for harboring such superstitious and ignorant thoughts, and he began to experience the joy of living. He began to affirm: "God's love united us. I see the Presence of God in my wife and she sees the Presence of God in me. Whenever I think of her I will affirm, 'God loves you and cares for you.'" Their marriage is now growing more blessed through the years. He was healed of a false, superstitious belief.

THE COSMIC ENERGIZER GOD DOES NOT PUNISH

Self-forgiveness is harmony and peace of mind. Self-condemnation and self-criticism mean misery and suffering. The Cosmic Energizer is the Life-Principle animating all things. If you burn yourself, the Life-Principle reduces the edema, giving you new skin and bone. Life holds no grudge against you. If you cut yourself, the Life-Principle builds a bridge of new cells and proceeds to heal you. If you should eat some tainted food, the Life-Principle forgives you and causes you to regurgitate the food. It always seeks to heal and restore you to wholeness.

If you misused the principles of chemistry or mathematics and then began to use these principles correctly, you would get immediate correct results. Likewise, when you begin to use your mind correctly by straight-line thinking, i.e., thinking from the standpoint of eternal verities, which are the same yesterday, today and forever, your subconscious will respond immediately to the new pattern, and the past will be forgotten and remembered no more.

A HARLOT FINDS A HAPPY MARRIAGE

A few years ago a woman "following the primrose path" said to me, "I have been reading *The Power of Your Subconscious Mind** and I want to lead a new life, get married, be respectable and have a home of my own and children. What shall I do? Am I condemned?"

I explained to her that the minute she came to a clear-cut decision and sincerely desired to be what she wanted to be, the Almighty Power would move on her behalf, brining the cherished desires of her heart to pass. I emphasized the simple truth that God (the Life-Principle)—the Cosmic Energizer—condemns no one.—*Thou art of purer eyes than to behold evil, and canst not look on iniquity* . . . (Habakkuk 1:13). Society and the world may criticize, or you may engage in self-accusation and self-criticism.—*For the Father judgeth no man, but hath committed all judgment unto the son* (John 5:22). The son is your mind. This is the place wherein you pronounce judgment on yourself by the thoughts you entertain. You forgive yourself by giving yourself moods of peace, love and harmony.

I suggested to this woman that all she had to do was to

**The Power of Your Subconscious Mind* by Dr. Joseph Murphy, Prentice-Hall, Inc., Englewood Cliffs, N.J., 1963.

turn away from the past and to unite mentally and emotionally with her aims in life, which are peace, dignity, marriage, happiness and freedom. As she continued to do this, God and His love would respond. Furthermore, I added that as she continued to do this, a wave of peace would move over the arid areas of her mind like the dew of heaven, and all the shadows of fear and guilt would be pushed away. As she ceased to condemn herself, the world would cease to condemn her.

The Prayer That Changed Her Life

She used this prayer frequently: "I forgive myself completely, and any time I am prone to criticize myself, I will affirm, 'I exalt God in the midst of me.' God loves me and cares for me. His peace fills my soul, and His love saturates my whole being. I am now married in my mind to a spiritual-minded man and there are harmony, peace and understanding between us. I give thanks for my happy marriage, my wonderful home and my two children."

Her inner speech and conversation were the same as if she were already objectively married and had a home and children. All that she desired came to pass, and she is now living a noble, God-like life today. She married a professional man, has a lovely home and gave birth to twins.

You Can Experience Happiness in Marriage

Happiness in marriage depends on love, loyalty, devotion to truth, integrity and a desire to lift up each other spiritually, mentally and in all ways. Love does not take a woman to a shabby, third-rate motel; neither is real love expressed furtively by an illicit interlude in some cheap hotel off the beaten path. To maintain a happy married life, pray together and you will stay together.

Affirm frequently: "Divine love, harmony, peace, and perfect understanding are now operating and experienced in our heavenly marriage. Morning, noon and night we salute the Divinity in each other and all our ways are ways of pleasantness and all our paths are of peace."

POINTS TO REMEMBER

1. Marriage, to be real, must first be on a spiritual basis. Each partner must have a reverence for the Divinity that shapes our ends. Love must unite two hearts as one. A rabbi, priest or minister does not validate a marriage; marriage is consecrated within the hearts of two people.

2. Like attracts like. In order to attract the right man in your life, you must dwell on the characteristics and qualities you admire in a man. As you think of these qualities with interest, like seeds, these qualities will sink into your subconscious and you will attract the embodiment of your ideal, based on the law. All seeds grow after their kind.

3. It is an excellent idea to sit down quietly and ask yourself honestly: "What do I have to give a man?" Think of all your wonderful qualities, talents and abilities and let that be your broadcast; you will find there is a man somewhere who will receive your broadcast. All of us

are receiving and broadcasting, mentally speaking, and what you are seeking is always seeking you.

4. If a man is seeking a wife, he should dwell on the qualities he admires in a woman; then, by contemplating these characteristics and qualities, they will become subjectified and the infinite intelligence of his subconscious mind will bring both of them together in Divine order.

5. Marriage is the holiest of all earthly institutions. It should be entered into reverently, thoughtfully and with a deep understanding of its spiritual significance. Marriage is an accord of Divine ideas, a harmony and purity of purpose.

6. Many men and women, many of whom are grandfathers and grandmothers, widowers and widows, have found joy and happiness in attracting companionship into their lives. In many the fires of sex have diminished entirely, but they are honest, sincere and just with each other, and their marriages are also of love because justice, honesty, integrity and thoughtfulness are all children of love. Love, kindness, truth, beauty, harmony and peace know no age. They are timeless, ageless and eternal.

7. Divorce is an individual matter and cannot be generalized. Divorce may be the only answer in some instances and completely wrong in others. There is no stigma attached to a divorce. Many divorced women are far more noble, honest and God-like than many of their friends and relatives who would rather live a lie in marriage than face the truth.

8. When a woman is tricked and deceived in marriage and finds that her spouse is a wife-beater, a nonprovider, a dope addict or trafficker in the same, she should immediately dissolve the lie, as, in reality, no marriage has taken place.

9. Men and women in the Bible represent the interaction of your conscious (husband) and your subconscious (wife). The union of these two determines all your experiences, conditions and events. If a man gives allegiance, loyalty and devotion to the Cosmic Energizer, which is the God-Presence within, he will automatically be faithful to his wife, his employer, his children and his country. The word *adultery* in the Bible is taken from idolatry, i.e., worshipping false gods such as giving power to the stars, the weather, other people, conditions, circumstances, etc.; or, if one believes in two powers or a devil, he is committing adultery and cohabiting with evil in the bed of his mind. There is only One Power—not two, three or a thousand—just One. Also, if he cohabits with remorse, self-condemnation, resentment, anger, hate or hostility, he is also committing adultery and fornication, which really means the same thing. Of course, he is already divorced because he is separated in his mind from love, peace, harmony, joy, honesty and goodwill. Adultery and fornication are of the mind. The body moves as it is moved upon; the body acts as it is acted upon. Divorce takes place in the mind first.

10. The Cosmic Energizer, or Life Principle, never condemns or punishes. We do this to ourselves by misuse of the law of our subconscious, by negative thinking and

by misinterpretation of life. Love knows no creed, dogma, race, nation or color. Love transcends all these things. God is love, and no respecter of persons.

11. Self-forgiveness is harmony and peace of mind. Self-condemnation is misery and suffering. The Life Principle is forever forgiving you, whether you burn or cut yourself or take some poisonous food. Your mind is a principle, and if you misused the principle of chemistry for 50 years and then began to use it in the right way, you would get immediate correct results. The same is true of your mind-principle. Begin to think right, feel right, act right, do right and pray right and you will receive an automatic response from your subconscious and the past will be forgotten and remembered no more. All you have to do is to forgive yourself and then resolve not to repeat the errors.

12. A harlot who ceases to criticize and condemn herself, and decides definitely to lead a new and wonderful life, and who contemplates regularly and systematically the truths of God, when she really comes to a clear-cut decision to lead a full and happy life, finds the subconscious will respond accordingly. One such woman, who realized there was no God up there in the sky who was going to punish her, but that she was the cause of all that was happening to her, decided to change completely and to lead a new life in God, to marry and have a home and children; so, according to her decision was it done unto her. She discovered that when she ceased to condemn herself, there was no one who condemned her. —*Woman, where are those thine accusers? Hath no man*

*condemned thee? She said, No man, Lord . . . Neither do I
condemn thee: go, and sin no more* (John 8:10,11).

13. Happiness in marriage depends on love, loyalty, devo-
    tion to truth, integrity and a desire to lift up one another
    spiritually, mentally and all ways. To maintain a happy
    married life, pray together and you will stay together.

14

How the Cosmic Energizer Gives Endless Supply Through Thought-Images

AN ARTICLE APPEARED in the September 5, 1973 issue of *The Wall Street Journal* by Richard James, one of their staff reporters. I am going to condense it here to illustrate a point.

WALL, SOUTH DAKOTA, HAS POPULATION OF ONLY 800, BUT ITS DRUGSTORE DRAWS 10,000 A DAY

Mr. Hustead bought the store in 1931 for $2,500. Business wasn't good. The first month's gross was $350. Fearing he couldn't maintain a home and make the grade in those depression days, he curtained off the back 20 feet of the store and moved in with his wife, Dorothy, and their 4-year-old son, Bill. This was their home for six years.

His wife undoubtedly wanted her husband to prosper, and when you are looking for a creative idea your subconscious will always respond. The idea came to her to offer free ice water to hot, dusty motorists if they would stop. They did and the thought-image that came to her mind caused the Wall

Drug Store to prosper beyond their fondest dreams. The store now attracts some 10,000 customers a day during the tourist season and does more than a million dollars worth of business a year. The drug store occupies an acre of space, and in the summer employs 150 people working seven days a week in two shifts from 5:00 a.m. to 10:00 p.m.

The thought-image in her mind was instant supply. You too can have an idea worth a fortune right now.

How Disciplined Imagination Brings Success

William Harriman imagined a railroad across America. With pen and paper he traced the imaginary line across the continent. The image he had in his mind was backed up by faith and confidence. It revolutionized industry and commerce and put millions to work, making untold fortunes for others.

How Imagination Made Him a Multimillionaire

Imagination is the action of forming mental images or concepts of what is not actually present to the senses. A number of years ago in an article in *Everybody's Magazine*, Henry M. Flagler, the Standard Oil multimillionaire, stated that the master secret of his success and his immense wealth was his capacity to image a thing as a finished form. In other words, he imagined the end, the final result, and all the forces of the Cosmic Energizer came to his aid. He actually visioned the whole project as completed.

He would close his eyes and imagine the tracks on the ground, the trains running and steaming, and the men going to work talking and laughing. He would imagine that he heard the train whistles blowing. He imagined the whole scene with a remarkable sensory vividness, imagining and feeling the reality of the finished project until it became natural to him; then, having impregnated his subconscious mind, all the forces of the Infinite came to his aid, and by the law of attraction he became an irresistible magnet attracting to him all those who aided him in the fulfillment of his dream.

THE WONDERS OF DISCIPLINED, CONTROLLED AND DIRECTED IMAGINATION

The late Dr. Fenwicke Holmes, author, lecturer, and brother of the late Dr. Ernest Holmes, told me about his friend, Arthur E. Stillwell, who had cultivated and disciplined his imagination to a high degree. He said that Stillwell had built more miles of railroad than any other man of his time and that all his accomplishments were the result of mental pictures which welled up from his deeper mind.

The most extraordinary incident happened in the building of the Kansas City and Southern Railroad. This railroad ends in the South at Port Arthur; however, the engineers preferred and suggested Galveston. Dr. Holmes said that an intuitive flash came to the mind of Arthur Stillwell in which he saw the disaster which later overtook Galveston. A tidal wave struck, which would have destroyed the terminal had it been placed there.

The wise use of his imagination and the laws of his subconscious saved him and his associates from a tragic mistake.

His subconscious responded to his faith and confidence in a guiding principle that knows all and sees all.

THE REASON HE DID NOT GET RESULTS

A manager of a large concern said to me that he mentally affirmed that he had a lovely home, wealth, and promotion in his business but that he was getting nowhere. He had a desire for the riches of life, but unfortunately he had the acquired habit of imagining financial lack all his life. His images of poverty and lack were greater than his belief and expectancy in wealth.

I explained to him what Emile Coué, the French psychologist, taught years ago: "Whenever the will (your desire) and the imagination are in conflict, the imagination always wins." In other words, you don't coerce or compel your subconscious mind; it is best acted upon by mental pictures. The Chinese say that one picture is worth a thousand words. Coué gave the vivid explanation of pointing out that a man will easily walk a plank on the ground because his desire to do so and his imagination are in agreement; but when the same plank is elevated in the air and placed between two buildings, and the same man is asked to walk it, though it is his desire to walk it, he has a mental picture of falling, and usually his picture of falling wins the day.

Your subconscious accepts the dominant of two ideas.

HOW HE AVOIDED THE MENTAL CONFLICT

I asked him a simple question: "Do you agree that there is such a thing as wealth?" "Oh, yes," he said. "Everywhere I look I see wealth, and I also realize I can have an idea worth a fortune." I explained that his affirmation of wealth succeeds best when there is no conflict and that his subconscious accepts what he really imagines and feels to be true, not just idle statements or words.

Furthermore, he realized that his subconscious is like the soil: it will take any kind of seed (thought or image) given it and bring forth accordingly, and that he should live in the joyous expectancy of the best. In other words, he naturally expects a harvest after planting the corn, wheat or oats.

THE IDEAL TECHNIQUE FOR RECONCILING THE CONSCIOUS AND SUBCONSCIOUS MIND

With great sincerity he got his desire and his imagination to agree by entering into a drowsy, sleepy state, which brings all effort to a minimum. The conscious mind is submerged to a great extent when in a sleepy state. The best time to impregnate the subconscious is prior to sleep. The reason for this is that the highest degree of outcropping of the subconscious occurs prior to sleep and just after we awaken. In this state of mind the negative thoughts and imagery which tend to neutralize your desire and so prevent acceptance by your subconscious mind no longer present themselves.

He imaged wealth and success, and he made this practical affirmation frequently, particularly prior to sleep: "By day and by night I am advancing and growing, and I am being prospered in all my interests. My sales are improving every day. More and more money comes in every day. In this relaxed state, I now picture the lovely home I want; it is large and commodious. There is a beautiful garden. I walk in my imagination through the house; I water the garden. I mentally enter all the rooms, and I play in the den with my boys. I see in my mind's eye a beautiful rug on the floor, upholstered chairs and a piano for my wife. I am now living in this house in my imagination and enjoying its beauty and comfort. In my imagination I am counting large sums of money, and I am mentally depositing large amounts in the bank. The bank manager is congratulating me. I live the role in my mind and enjoy the sensory vividness and reality of it all."

He kept this scenic drama up regularly and systematically two or three times a day and made sure he did not subsequently deny or negate the mental movie. At the end of two months his dream was realized. He inherited a home which met all his requirements and coincided with his mental movie. His mother, who lived a half mile away, passed away suddenly in her sleep, bequeathing everything, including her beautiful home, to her son. The estate was worth over $400,000.

His subconscious responded to his relaxed affirmations and silent imagery and brought results in ways he could never conceive of with his conscious, reasoning mind. He was also made general manager of the organization where he was employed.—*And all things, whatsoever ye shall ask in prayer, believing, ye shall receive* (Matthew 21:22).

How Imagination Releases Dynamic Energy

A businessman complained to me that he was always tired, that he had that all-gone feeling accompanied by depression. However, it was not his body that was tired; it was his mental attitude. I explained to him that it was not the work but his thoughts about his work that exhausted him, and that it is the mind that gets tired due to his habitual thoughts of anxiety, fear, resentment, jealousy and suppressed rage.

He revised the procedure forthwith and began to affirm: "The Cosmic Energizer flows through me vitalizing, energizing and renewing my entire being. I am inspired from On High. I am vital, enthusiastic, and full of goodwill to all. I bless and pour out benedictions on all my associates, and I exalt God in the midst of me."

As he continued to do this, he found a constant flow of energy developed, and he ceased thinking negatively. He imagined the president of the company congratulating him, shaking hands with him, mentioning that he was promoted with a large increase in salary, knowing that what he subjectively imagined, claimed and felt to be true would come to pass. He began to think, imagine, speak and act in exactly the same way he would were he already promoted with a large increase in income.

He learned that by employing inner speech, your inner conversation with yourself, plus imagining the happy ending is the way to bring things to pass on the screen of space. A few months went by, and he was lifted out of his present position and made executive vice president at double his previous salary, accompanied with other emoluments.

A Young Boy Discovered How
His Imagination Released Energy

A young man from Canada spent some time with his uncle in Los Angeles one summer. One day, his uncle said, he complained of being so exhausted, tired and depressed that he did not feel like even watering the garden; it seemed actually too much effort to lift the hose. Walking seemed to be somewhat of a struggle. In a few hours' time, though, a young girl appeared with a tennis racket and asked him to come along for a game. All of a sudden a surge of energy seized him, a new light came into his eyes, and he began to bubble over with enthusiasm. After the tennis game he took her to a dance and got home about midnight full of life and love.

He had been tired in his thoughts because his girlfriend in Canada wrote him stating that she was dating another boy in his home town. Once another vision of beauty and charm came into his life, he changed his thought, releasing enormous energy and vitality. Energy is siphoned off by unhealthy, depressing thoughts. Think of faith, love, and goodwill to all and your whole physiological system will respond.

The boy's images of doing what he loved to do, accompanied by an attractive young lady, gave him instantaneous energy.

RELEASE YOUR ENERGY

Sir Thomas Buxton said: "The longer I live, the more deeply am I convinced that that which makes the difference between one man and another—between the weak and powerful, the great and insignificant—is energy: invisible determination, a purpose once formed; then death or victory. This quality will do anything that is to be done in the world, and no talent, no circumstance, no opportunity will make one a man without it."

Johann von Goethe said: "Energy will do anything that can be done in the world, and no talent, no circumstance, no opportunity will make a two-legged person a man without it."

How the Cosmic Energizer Found the Purchaser

At the beginning of creation, the Cosmic Energizer brought forth all things in the universe through creative imagination. The universal language of the Cosmic Energizer or Infinite Spirit (God) is the language of mental images. God imagined man, and God became what He imagined Himself to be. The Cosmic Energizer starts the idea for a world and galaxies in space. It visions suns, moons and stars and all things therein contained in this limitless cosmos and all Its dreams come to pass. It becomes the thing It imagines Itself to be.

This same vitality of Divine imagination is in every man. I spoke along the above lines to a widow, who was trying to sell her apartment building after her husband had passed on. She was in financial trouble, she had many vacancies, some tenants had not paid the rent, and the neighborhood was changing. She was afraid she would have to declare bankruptcy. The building was in the hands of brokers, but she had received no offers.

I explained to her that what she was seeking was also seeking her and that the Intelligence of the Cosmic Energizer would attract the right purchaser. She prayed as follows: "Infinite Intelligence knows where the right purchaser is, and he is Divinely directed to this apartment building. He wants it and he prospers in it. There is a Divine exchange, and we are both satisfied."

At my suggestion she also used her imaginative faculty and began to dramatize in her mind a buyer coming into her office and expressing an interest in her property. She imagined him saying to her, "I will buy it." She enacted this scenic dream several times a day, making sure that her mental imagery agreed with her affirmation of the truth. A few days after practicing this technique, a man came, looked it over, and seemed interested, but told her the next day that the price was too high.

THERE IS A RIGHT AND A WRONG WAY TO PRAY

She asked me to pray with her that this man would buy the apartment building. I explained to her that that would be the wrong approach and that she should never use mental coercion to force a sale, as that would be an invasion of the right of the buyer. I explained that Infinite Intelligence knows where the right buyer is and that he would want and desire her building; that there was no acceptable occasion to *make* him want it, and that she must realize that faith in the workings of her deeper mind would bring right results. We work by faith; not by hypnotizing others to do what we want.

THE ANSWER WAS NEXT DOOR TO HER

The man who had rejected the building told his medical doctor about it, since his physician was looking for a good investment. This medical doctor lived in the next building to hers. He quickly bought the building and was delighted with the purchase. All her problems were solved.

—If thou canst believe, all things are possible to him that belie-veth (Mark 9:23).

POINTS TO REMEMBER

1. A pharmacist bought a store in Wall, South Dakota, for $2500. His income was $350 a month, and financially he could not make ends meet. His wife had an idea worth a fortune, however. She urged her husband to put signs along the highway offering ice water to slake the thirst of motorists. Her idea resulted in a million dollar business and 10,000 customers a day. You too can have an idea or thought-image worth a fortune. Wealth is a thought-image in the mind—nothing more or less.

2. Some years ago in *Everybody's Magazine* there appeared an article showing the tremendous power of imagination backed by faith. Henry M. Flagler became a multimillionaire through the disciplined, controlled and directed image in his mind. He knew there was oil in a certain area, and he imagined the derricks, the train tracks, and the men going to and fro. Actually, in his vivid imagination he even heard the whistles blow, saw the steam and the whole project in completion. He ran this mental movie over and over in his mind until it became so natural and real that he impregnated his subconscious with his mental image; then, by the law of attraction, everything he needed was provided. Everything in the world you look at was first a thought-image or an idea in the mind of man or the mind of God, and there is only One Mind common to all individual men.

3. Arthur Stillwell cultivated his imagination to an extraordinary degree. He visualized the building of the Kansas City and Southern Railroad, but when the best engineers recommended Galveston instead of Port Arthur for the terminus, he insisted on Port Arthur. His intuitive faculty was developed to a high degree by visualizing the project in detail, while realizing at the same time that there was an infinite intelligence in his subconscious mind guiding and directing him in all his ways. An intuitive flash revealed to him that a tidal wave would destroy Galveston, and the inner promptings of his deeper mind proved true.

4. Many pray for wealth, success and prosperity, and at the same time have the image of lack and limitation. The desire and the imagination must agree. When your desire and your imagination are in conflict, your imagination always wins. A simple way to overcome this and get your conscious and subconscious to agree is by affirming: "By day and by night I am advancing and moving forward, and I am being prospered in all my ways. My sales are improving every day, and I am receiving more and more money every day." There will be no argument in the conscious or subconscious mind concerning the preceding statement, as any man will admit he can learn a little more every day, he can sell more every day, he can attract more customers every day, and he can make more money every day.

5. The minute you admit there is such a thing as wealth, which you see everywhere, you will have no problem in

living in the joyous expectancy of God's riches—spiritual, mental and material.

6. An excellent way to get a promotion and have a lovely home or a car is to relax your mind and get into a sleepy, drowsy state, a state akin to sleep, since this brings about an outcropping of your subconscious mind and all effort and negative thoughts are reduced to a minimum. In that state think, imagine, speak and act the way you would as if you possessed a beautiful home, were already promoted, possessed a wonderful new car, etc. Picture the ideal home in your mind, walk through the house, water the garden, and play with the children in your mind. Make it vivid and real. Feel the naturalness of it, feel the solidity of the walls and the furniture. Show your friends through the house. Live there mentally and what you imagine and feel to be true will come to pass. You can do the same thing for a car, a promotion, or anything else. All transactions take place in the mind. This is the meaning of believe (live in the state of being it), you have it now (in your mind it is real), and then you shall objectify it on the screen of space.

7. Negative thoughts of fear, depression, anger, resentment, etc. siphon off vital energy resulting in that all gone feeling of tiredness and general lassitude. Reverse your thoughts and think on harmony, love, peace, joy and goodwill, and you will release tremendous energy and will be inspired from On High. Claim that the vitalizing, healing, energizing power of the Cosmic Energizer is flowing through you and you will be renewed

and regenerated. A boy who is complaining and whining about being tired doing work in the garden, and who suddenly is visited by a vision of loveliness and charm in the form of a girl with a tennis racket, who wished him to play with her, is suddenly seized with enormous energy and seems to be transformed by a transfusion from On High. His tiredness was due to the news that his girl friend in Canada was going with another boy. When this was supplanted by imagining a wonderful game of tennis with a beautiful young woman, the energy of the Infinite was released.

8. The Cosmic Energizer imagined the world, suns, moons, stars and all things therein contained, and It became what It imagined Itself to be. This quality of imagination is in every person. A widow who had difficulty selling her apartment house and who was in financial straits imagined that she was showing the apartment to the right buyer, who wanted it and who would prosper in it. She went through the mental movie several times a day, showing him the several apartments, records, income, and hearing him say clearly and distinctly in her imagination: "I will buy it." After a short while she attracted a local doctor, who wanted the building, and this resolved her problem.

9. You must not try to make a person buy a building by hypnotic suggestion; neither do you use any subtle mental influence praying that he will purchase it. This would be an invasion of his rights. On the contrary, you trust the infinite intelligence of your subconscious to attract to you the right buyer at the right time and in the right

way. It makes no mistakes. It is also completely wrong to pray that that man or that woman will marry you. Trust the infinite intelligence to bring your desires to pass; then there is no occasion for mental coercion or trying to influence others to do your bidding.

15

How the Cosmic Energizer Can Quickly Turn Your Dreams Into Reality

THE LIFE-PRINCIPLE (which is God) is always seeking expression through you. The whole movement of life is from the invisible to the visible, from your thought to its manifestation, from your dream or ideal to actualization, from the subjective to the objective. The inexhaustible, limitless fountain of possibilities and potentialities is within you now, waiting for you to bring all your dreams into reality. You are here to express the riches of life in all possible dimensions and directions. You are here to express the joy of living life more abundantly. The Divine Presence is seeking to express Itself in form and function through your brain, your hands and through the words of your mouth. It is impossible for you to exhaust the infinite riches of your subconscious mind.

DAY-DREAMING IS AN ESCAPE FROM REALITY

Many people indulge in day-dreaming, wherein they engage in fantasizing something pleasant, while nevertheless believing it could never happen to them because they think it is too good to be true. This attitude is actually a pure waste of time and results in debilitating the entire mentality. You must realize that there is nothing too good to be true, and nothing too wonderful to last, for the love, the light, the glory and the riches of the Cosmic Energizer are the same yesterday, today and forever.

How Her Dream of a Balkan Tour Came to Pass

The author took a tour of Yugoslavia with a group of 60 people during the month of October 1973. We had two special guides and two special buses, which traversed all the major cities and many of the historical landmarks. One young lady who sat next to me in one of the restaurants was from San Francisco. She had been working in a legal office when she saw an advertisement in a magazine about a special Yugoslavian tour. She read that Yugoslavia is characterized mainly by its numerous contrasts: a wide variety of religions, languages, traditions, customs and folklore. She was intensely interested in the fact that so many different cultures were to be encountered in this relatively small country. She said to me, "I wanted to go, but I didn't have the money."

How She Used the Cosmic Energizer

However, it turned out that this young legal secretary was given a copy of *The Power of Your Subconscious Mind.** She

---

*The Power of Your Subconscious Mind by Dr. Joseph Murphy, Prentice-Hall, Inc., Englewood Cliffs, N.J., 1963.

began to read it avidly, and every night before she went to sleep, she began to imagine herself seated on a plane. She felt the rhythm of the engines. She felt the plane lift off the ground and she conducted an imaginary conversation with a hostess. She centered her imagination on being *in* the airplane and on viewing San Francisco from her imaginary aerial ride. She thought and imaged from the ride, feeling the reality and joy of it all.

She continued this mental journey every night for about a week. Her expectancy and deep desire were emotionally joined together, and they passed into her subconscious mind and became a physical reality.

How the Answer Came

A wealthy woman, a client who came to her boss for legal advice, while waiting in the office, began to chat with her. The secretary casually mentioned that she had read about a trip to Yugoslavia and how she would love to go but would have to wait until she had accumulated sufficient money. This client of her boss said, "How strange. I am going on that trip. I would love to have you come along as my guest and companion." She accepted immediately, as she knew this was an answer to her prayer.—*Believe that ye receive them, and ye shall have them* (Mark 11:24).

The Wise Use of Imagination

The answer to your desire depends upon the intensity of your imagination and not upon external facts. Where the five-sense man sees an acorn, the man with disciplined imagination sees an oak tree. As man awakens to the imaginative life, he discovers that to imagine and feel the reality of his desire makes it so. Man's outer world and all its happenings, experiences and events are projections of his inner mental images. When man becomes conscious of his inner causal world of imagination and the outer world of effects, he begins to bring his desires to fulfillment.

How His Dream of Perfect Health Came True

The following letter is from Mr. William H. Thrall, a distinguished educator of San Gabriel, Southern California. Mr. Thrall has written and said that I have his complete permission to write this article about his remarkable healing:

I had an experience myself that I rarely talk about. When I was young—about nine years old—I fell a couple of stories through the chimney opening of a partially constructed house. I broke an arm and cracked my skull. I bled profusely. I was unconscious for a week. The doctors gave me up for lost. They didn't even set my arm. Why bother? My mother was beside me day and night praying. One night, she told me later, I said, "I see angels all around me." It must have wrung her heart. A week after the accident I woke up, quickly regained my health and have now almost reached the age of sixty. God must have had a purpose for me, and it is true, I have affected many lives for the better during my many years in the field of education.

How He Discovered the Wonders of the Cosmic Energizer

During our visit to Yugoslavia, we visited Plitvice, noted for its lakes, which are of indescribable beauty with their waterfalls, travertine barriers, caves, vegetation, vast, well-preserved woods, primeval mountain forests and excellent trout fishing. While conversing with one of the residents of the area whom I met in the Jezero Hotel, he told me that he was a veteran of the Second World War. He had returned to his own home in this area and was receiving a pension from the United States Government. When he retired to Yugoslavia, he felt that his income was somewhat inadequate, inasmuch as he had married since leaving the U.S. Army and now had two children.

He had studied mental and spiritual laws in the United States, however, and began to apply what he had learned. He told me that his most pressing desire was to acquire a substantial income in order to maintain his home comfortably and to provide adequately for the education of his children.

The Technique That Brought Results from the Cosmic Energizer

He followed this procedure every night just before he fell asleep: In his imagination he began to feel that he was teaching English to a group of executives and businessmen. He felt the naturalness of it and the thrill of accomplishment. He did this faithfully, knowing that he would inevitably get an answer. It came as no surprise when, after a few months, a director of a large company asked him if he would be willing to join his organization and teach the key men conversational English, because they made frequent trips to the United States, England, Canada and Australia. Today, at a substantially higher income, and with the assurance of continued progress, he travels with members of his organization to English-speaking countries and is deeply respected and appreciated.

This man, a native of Yugoslavia, who had lived many years in the United States, had heard the late Dr. Emmett Fox say, "When you pray, instead of thinking of the end desired, think from the end." In other words, imagine the reality of your desire now and live the role in your imagination. Your inner action must correspond to the action you would physically perform after realizing your desire.

A Visit to Sarejevo and Some Consultations

Sarejevo, the name of the city which reminds us of that fatal event in June 1914, which plunged Europe into the whirlpool of the First World War, is today the cultural, economic and political center of the Socialist Republic of Bosnia and Herzegovina, its capital. This is the third city in Yugoslavia and is a university center which harbors 30,000 students. It was here at the Bristol Hotel where I met and had a conference with two tourists who were traveling with different organizations than our group.

He Was Blaming Providence for His Troubles

One of the tourists from New York who was taking a private, conducted tour of Yugoslavia, on hearing I was a minister, asked for a conference. During the interview he said that he was very unhappy and dissatisfied, that his wife had left him for another man and that his two sons were in jail in New York for selling dope. He asked why God was punishing him, as he went to church, gave to charities, had been good to his wife and worked hard.

I explained to him that it is foolish and useless to blame Providence for his troubles or to endeavor to place the responsibility upon other people. The whole cosmos is governed in accordance with law, for God, among other things, is Principle, or Law, and where Law obtains there can be no room for casting blame on God or others.

If you break the laws of your mind or any other law, you suffer the consequences, and that is all there is to it. It is merely a question of cause and effect. When you use your mind correctly and harmoniously, it is your guarantee of victory, freedom and peace of mind.

I continued to explain to him that the Cosmic Energizer was seeking expression through him and that all he had to do was to cause himself to become a clear, open channel. If, on the other hand, he should become resentful, full of self-condemnation, morbid and angry, then he would be obstructing the flow of the Cosmic Energizer, the Life Force, and would become frustrated, dammed up, and all sorts of stress, strain and ill effects would follow.

How He Learned to Release the Imprisoned Splendor

This man realized that his business here on this plane of life is to be a channel for the Divine Spiritual Energy, which is referred to in this book as the Cosmic Energizer. When he does this, wonders happen in his life and all his dreams come to pass.

There is only one Cosmic Energy in the cosmos, but we can use this energy constructively or destructively, because man has the unique capacity to choose. When we use this Cosmic Energizer constructively and harmoniously, we experience harmony, health, peace and improve our lives in every possible way. When we use it destructively, we damage ourselves, retard our progress, bring on sickness and failure, and waste our opportunities to bless mankind.

THE PRAYER THAT TRANSFORMED HIS LIFE

He used the following prayer morning, afternoon and night, knowing that these spiritual vibrations would permeate his whole being and enter into his subconscious mind, obliterating all the negative patterns previously lodged therein:

> I am a channel for the Divine Energy. God flows through me as harmony, health, peace, joy, wholeness, beauty and abundance. I am Divinely guided in all ways. Divine right action is mine. Divine love fills my soul. Divine peace saturates my mind and heart. I surrender my wife to God and I wish for her all the blessings of life. God guides my boys and God gives them freedom and peace of mind. Whenever I think of my wife or children I will immediately affirm, "God loves you and cares for you." Whenever a negative thought enters my mind, I will immediately supplant it and affirm, "God loves me and cares for me."

A month had passed by since I first met him. Then came a letter from him saying that when he returned home to New York, his wife was there waiting for him, and asking his forgiveness. There was a joyous reunion. His two boys have given up dope, have been released from prison, and are studying along spiritual lines in New York City. He truly discovered that wonders happen as you pray.

SHE CHANGED HER ATTITUDE AND REALIZED HER DESIRE

An elderly woman on the same tour as the previously mentioned man came to my room in the Bristol Hotel for an interview. Her problem was that she had loaned $10,000 to her brother in order for him to pay off a business debt. Her brother gave her a promissory note at 6 percent interest to be paid back in two years. When the first year term expired, he failed to meet his interest payments, but promised to pay 60 days later. This he also failed to do. His wife had said to her, "You are rich. You will never get your money back."

This woman was very resentful and very angry, because her brother would not even answer her phone calls or respond to her letters. She told me that she hated to sue her own brother and start a legal battle; moreover, she believed that her sister-in-law was really the stumbling block. She knew her brother's business was prospering and that he was able to pay.

I said to her that she can never lose anything except she accepts the loss in her mind, as all transactions take place through the mind. You gain through mental acceptance of your good, and you can lose only through the mental acceptance of loss. Furthermore, I pointed out to her that she must never mentally deprive or deny others of their ability to pay by saying, "He has the money and he won't pay me." "He pays others but not his sister." "His wife is preventing him from paying me." "I'll never get it back," etc.

As a matter of fact, she had been robbing her brother of his ability and willingness to pay her what he owed her. I suggested that she change her attitude completely and to stop giving power to her sister-in-law, but instead to give her allegiance and loyalty to the Cosmic Energizer within, which is omnipotent and supreme. I wrote down for her a simple technique or prayer process which she agreed to follow every night and also during the day, if she so desired. Following is the prayer:

My brother is God's man. God is prospering him in all ways. He meets all his obligations in Divine order. There are harmony, peace, love and understanding between us. I now construct an imaginary scene and hear my brother's voice saying, "Sis, I am paying you back in full."

For six consecutive nights she conducted this imaginary drama. In her recent letter to me from New York City, she advised that she had received a telephone call from her brother saying that he was sorry about the delay in payment but that she would receive the $10,000 back plus interest the next day, which she did.

The ancients called imagination the workshop of God. Use your imagination to achieve your particular dream or aspiration. Clearly define and imagine the particular end. Feel the reality of the fulfilled desire and the result will follow.

When you imagine the particular end, you are discriminating clearly. How do you distinguish the apple tree from the pine tree, or the donkey from the horse, but by the clearly defined image and outline in your mind.

HOW A JEWELER MADE HIS DREAM COME TRUE

Recently I visited Dubrovnik, the most beautiful city on the Adriatic, which offers the traveler pleasure of its great works of art, and is called one of the great gems of the Adriatic Coast. This city is noted for its marvelous architectural and sculptural works, and is looked upon as a tourist's paradise. I visited a jeweler and bought some beautiful silver hand-made bracelets. The jeweler and I had a long conversation about conditions in Yugoslavia, and he said that his country has complete religious freedom. The average salary is between $150 to $200 a month, but a nice apartment costs only $40 a month. Food and clothing are also quite reasonable. He said that he was a Roman Catholic and that when he started business he was not making ends meet, but that every morning he would go to the church and pray to the Virgin for prosperity and to show him the way to expand.

HOW THE ANSWER CAME

One day a jeweler from Canada came in, admired the beautiful silver bracelets and said to him, "These would sell in Montreal in a wonderful way," and he bought $1000 worth, stating that though he would have to pay duty on them in Canada, he would still make an excellent profit. With the passage of years this Canadian customer has recommended him to many others and his business has boomed. He said that in one year's time he was able to buy a new German car, a new home and hire some extra help.

This man believed that the Virgin (your subconscious mind) would answer his prayer, and his subconscious mind responded according to his belief. He did not understand that he actually answered his own prayer. *And all things, whatsoever ye shall ask in prayer, believing, ye shall receive* (Matthew 21:22). This applies whether the object of your faith be true or false. In this jeweler's instance, he had what we call blind faith.

How My Desire Came to Pass

In Belgrade I desired to visit some psychics to see how they perform. Our guide was not too cooperative, but there is always a way. I claimed that Infinite Intelligence would open up the door for me in Divine order. I was guided to a certain store, where I bought several gifts for our hostesses. I said to the owner that I was interested in ESP and psychic phenomena and that I was a writer. He arranged to go with me to visit his friend. He spoke excellent English, but the psychic spoke in her native tongue.

She read the contents of a letter which I had received that morning from Beverly Hills, and which I had not yet opened. This is clairvoyance. The businessman who accompanied me translated everything she said. She read my past, gave my occupation, and named all my close relatives, who she said were in Spirit land, all of which was very accurate. She gave the names of 36 books which I have written and gave the name of the radio station over which I broadcast. In a deep trance state she said, "Your brother, Thaddeus, is here." Then the tone of her voice changed and my brother's voice sounded natural and real. He gave the date of his transition and spoke of our early childhood. He spoke of the most intimate details. I asked him numerous questions about the family, and his life in the next dimension, all of which he answered with remarkable clarity, pointing out that his method of travel is thought and that when I went home to Beverly Hills there would be a special message from him.

Upon my return home, I am happy to say, I found a written note on my desk drawer saying, "I talked to you in Belgrade, and this is my signature." This was a very remarkable experience. In this instance, I do believe I was actually talking with my brother, and his signature was very familiar. Our loved ones are all around us, separated by frequency only.

How the Cosmic Energizer Made the Impossible Dream Possible

I requested an old friend of mine, Charles E. Lloyd, one of the most famous criminal attorneys on the West Coast, to give me the story of his rise from rags to riches. The following is his reply, which is a thrilling, absorbing and fascinating account of his rise to prominence and achievement:

I, Charles E. Lloyd, 625 Rimpau Boulevard, Los Angeles, California, give you permission to publish the story.

Route 1, Box 151 is the address of a 190-acre farm, four miles north of Indianola in the heart of Mississippi's Delta cotton belt.

There I chopped cotton from the age of eight, gave my pet roosters names of famous Americans—climbed mulberry and pecan trees to dream impossible dreams, and there I was molded, shaped and motivated by an amazing grandmother—widow of a freed slave—who wanted me to be a preacher.

Unfortunately, Grandmother Miller didn't live to see her young ward become "one of America's finest trial lawyers," as I was recently described.

It's a long, long way from Route 1, Box 151 Indianola, Mississippi to Hancock Park, California. I describe my journey as moving onward and upward. "God has placed before me this day an open door, which no man can shut."

I graduated from Indianola Colored High School in 1952 and the same year arrived with my family in Los Angeles with 12 cents, one pair of pants and a burning ambition to become a lawyer—a dream I had nurtured since visiting an attorney's office with my father as a nine-year-old.

Taking the Los Angeles police examination at the age of twenty, I was accepted for the Police Academy at twenty-one and graduated with the highest academic honors in my class. Then, while working full time as a Los Angeles police officer, I completed my last year of undergraduate work and attended law school. I received my bachelor's degree from Los Angeles State College and my law degree from the University of Southern California in 1961.

The next year the impossible dream was realized. I was appointed a deputy city attorney for the Los Angeles

City Attorney's Office. I served as chief prosecutor of the Criminal Division with a direct command of a staff of twenty-five lawyers.

I taught at Van Norman University. In April of 1964, I entered private practice and am now the senior partner of the firm of LLOYD, BRADLEY, BURRELL & Associates. My record as a defense attorney has been as spectacular as my role on the other side of the counsel table. I have handled some of the most publicized cases in all phases of law. I have represented some of the greatest stars in the entertainment field.

My ambition now is to become a Science of Mind minister and to affirm that the so-called disadvantaged can be inspired and motivated toward success and achievement through the power of the subconscious mind. I am now widely in demand as a public speaker and I am projecting a positive message.

I am now what I long to be.

This I believe . . . .

A man properly motivated can do the impossible because he doesn't know it can't be done.

POINTS TO REMEMBER

1. The Life Principle (which is God) is always seeking expression through you. The whole movement of life is from the invisible to the visible. You are here to express the joy of living. It is impossible for you to exhaust the limitless riches of the Cosmic Energizer within you.

2. Day-dreaming, believing that your dreams can't come to pass or are too good to be true, is a waste of time. Remember, there is nothing too good to be true, nothing too wonderful to last, for the riches of the Infinite are the same yesterday, today and forever. You must put foundations under your dream and realize and know that whatever you imagine and feel to be true will be deposited in your subconscious mind and come to pass in Divine order.

3. A young legal secretary had a great desire to go on a tour of Yugoslavia, but lacked the money. She was given a copy of *The Power of Your Subconscious Mind** and followed a technique outlined therein. Every night prior to sleep she imagined herself seated on the plane. She felt the rhythm of the engines and conducted an imaginary conversation with the stewardess. She centered her imagination on being on the airplane and viewing San Franscisco from her imaginary ride in the air. She continued this mental journey for a week, when on or about the eighth day, a client of her boss came into the office. As they chatted, she found that this woman was going to Yugoslavia and offered to take her along as a guest and companion, which she accepted.

4. The answer to your desire or dream of your heart depends on the intensity of your imagination, backed up by the realization that the Cosmic Energizer will move on your behalf, bringing it to pass in Divine order.

**The Power of Your Subconscious Mind* by Dr. Joseph Murphy, Prentice-Hall, Inc., Englewood Cliffs, N.J., 1963.

5. A veteran who had retired in Yugoslavia desired to increase his income and began to practice mental and spiritual laws which he had learned while living in the United States. Every night prior to sleep in his imagination he began to feel that he was teaching English to a group of executives and businessmen. He felt the naturalness of it all and the thrill of accomplishment. After a few months a director of a large corporation asked him to join the organization and teach the executives conversational English, as they made frequent business trips to English speaking countries. He thereby increased his income 400 percent in a year's time.

6. One of the tourists was blaming Providence for his troubles and believed that God was punishing him. He believed that was the reason his wife had deserted him and that his boys had become dope addicts. I explained to him the whole universe is governed by law and that the Cosmic Energizer (God) is no respecter of persons. When he used the Energy harmoniously and constructively, the result would be harmony, health, peace and abundance. All he had to do was to become a clear, open channel for the Divine Energy. He practiced the following prayer therapy three times a day: "I am a channel for the Divine Energy, which flows through me as harmony, health, peace, joy and abundance. I surrender my wife and boys to God completely, wishing for them all the blessings of life. Whenever I think of my wife or boys, I will immediately affirm, 'God loves you and cares for you.'" At the end of a month he wrote, stating that when he arrived home from his trip, his wife had

returned and his boys had given up dope. He discovered the wonders of the Cosmic Energizer within him.

7. A woman had loaned $10,000 to her brother, and the latter seemed unwilling to pay it back. She was resentful and highly critical of her brother and of his wife, who she suspected was the stumbling block in the repayment of the debt. I explained to her that she couldn't lose anything unless she admits the loss and that she must immediately cease depriving or denying her brother's ability to pay. She changed her attitude and affirmed frequently, "My brother is God's man. God is prospering him in all ways. He pays all his debts in Divine order. There are harmony, peace, love and understanding between us." She wrote me that within a week or so, her brother had phoned her and remitted the $10,000 plus the interest. Prayer always prospers.

8. A Yugoslavian jeweler who was not making ends meet visited the shrine of the Virgin every morning and prayed that the Virgin would prosper him and show him how to expand his business. The answer came through a Canadian businessman, who visited his shop and bought over $1000 worth of silver bracelets. He also recommended him to others, and the jeweler's business boomed 400 percent in one year. He prayed believingly, and his own subconscious mind brought it to pass in its own way. Every man answers his own prayer, for it is done unto us as we believe.

9. In Belgrade the author desired to see some psychics and mystics. There was reluctance on the part of the guides; however, the infinite intelligence of my subconscious

directed me to a shop where I made some purchases. The owner agreed to take me to his psychic, whom he consulted occasionally. She spoke in her native tongue and he translated what she said. In her trance state she read a letter in my pocket which I had not yet read. This is clairvoyance. She also read my entire history and my whole life was an open book to her. Through her, my brother communicated and spoke about the most intimate details of our early life together. I recognized his voice, its tonal qualities, and the Cork (Ireland) accent where he had lived all his life. He said that when I returned home, he would have a message waiting for me. I found a note with his signature in a drawer of my desk, saying, "I told you so." Our loved ones are all around us, separated by frequency only.

10. Charles E. Lloyd, famous criminal attorney, had a dream as a boy to become educated and an outstanding lawyer—this was a burning ambition. He nourished and sustained the idea, and having impregnated his subconscious mind, the latter caused him to take all the steps necessary to achieve his so-called impossible dream.

—Call unto me, and I will answer thee, and shew thee great and mighty things, which thou knowest not (Jeremiah 33:3).

16

The Cosmic Energizer Plan for Lifetime Abundance

—I am come that they might have life, and that they might have it more abundantly (John 10:10).

But my God shall supply all your need according to his riches in glory . . . (Philippians 4:19).

—God, who giveth us richly all things to enjoy (I Timothy 6:17).

O Son of Spirit, I have created thee rich.
How is it thou art poor?
And made thee mighty.
How is it thou art weak?
And from the very essence of love and wisdom
I have manifested thee.
How is it thou occupiest thyself with someone else?
Turn thy sight to thyself that thou mayest find me standing
in thee. Mighty—Powerful—Supreme.

—From the Hindu Scriptures

—The Lord shall open unto thee his good treasure, the heaven to give the rain unto thy land in his season, and to bless all the work of thine hand . . . (Deuteronomy 28:12).

THE DICTIONARY DEFINES *abundance* as an extreme or oversufficient quantity or supply: overflowing fullness, affluence, wealth, copiousness. Spiritually speaking, abundance means wave upon wave of prosperity, health, happiness, peace and all the blessings of life. God, or the Cosmic Energizer, is the

Source of our supply of energy, vitality, creative ideas, inspiration and wealth; and to keep in tune with the Infinite is the key to a lifetime of abundance which leads to a full and happy life.

I find in talking with many people that the reason they do not prosper is because they think it is wrong and sacrilegious to pray for wealth and success. Such an attitude is based on gross ignorance and superstition. Nothing could be further from the truth. These people believe in two powers, which is again too ridiculous for words.

There is only One Power, Cause and Substance, and that is the Cosmic Energizer. If there were two powers, one would cancel out the other and we would have a chaos instead of a cosmos. Mathematically, scientifically and spiritually there can be only One Power. There can't be two Infinites. Infinity cannot be divided or multiplied.

Those who hesitate to claim prosperity and the good things of life deprive themselves of these available and visible blessings. You are here to lead the life more abundant, and unless you express abundance and prosperity and claim the riches of the Infinite, you may find yourself besieged by creditors and even find your family in need.

This is a mental and spiritual universe, and the whole world is simply Spirit, God or the Cosmic Energizer in form. The Creator and the created are one. Spirit and matter are one. Modern science says that Energy (Spirit) and matter are interconvertible and interchangeable. The *Upanishads* said thousands of years ago that matter is the lowest degree of Spirit, and that Spirit is the highest degree of matter. Money may be looked upon as the visible manifestation of Invisible abundance.

Why She Did Not Prosper

Some time ago I talked with a young woman who was very attractive, personable, and highly educated and who had a very good position. However, she had not been promoted, yet other girls in the same department who were apparently less competent were promoted. She complained that the other girls in the office didn't like her, that she was not appreciated by her superior, and that men were jealous of her. I discovered during the conference, however, that her real trouble was that she looked down her nose at the other girls in the office. She said, "The men and the other girls in the office bore me," which meant that she looked down on them.

I explained to her that criticism and condemnation of others actually amounts to self-criticism and self-condemnation, for there is only one mind common to all individual men. I added that she was the only thinker in her universe and that she was responsible for her thoughts. Her depreciation of the other members of her department was actually self-depreciation. Her associates subconsciously picked up her vibrations, with the result that she lacked friends and had not been promoted once over a period of six years.

She Learned the Key to Abundance and Promotion in Life

This young lady learned that there is only one Cosmic Energy (Spirit) in the universe and that she is here to apply it constructively and harmoniously. She also became acutely aware of the fact that as long as she held thoughts of criticism and condemnation of others, she was using it destructively. All bitterness, resentment and spiritual pride are peculiarly destructive methods of misusing the Cosmic Energizer.

When we think negatively and destructively, our Divine Energy becomes dammed up in our subconscious mind, like placing your foot on the garden hose, producing lack, loss and limitation of all kinds.

SHE APPLIED THE LAW OF PROSPERITY AND CHANGED HER LIFE

Having learned why she was not promoted, she immediately reversed this attitude. I gave her the following prayer technique, explaining to her that she must have a general attitude of peace and goodwill toward all; that the universe is one, and that the law of harmony must prevail in her habitual thinking. Then, and then only, would she establish a clear, unobstructed flow of the Cosmic Energizer through her.

This is the prayer therapy she applied: "I am a daughter of the Infinite. God loves me and cares for me. I radiate love, peace and goodwill to all those in my office and to all people everywhere. I am Divinely guided and inspired. I know that God, or the Cosmic Energizer, is the source of my supply, and that all my needs are met at all times everywhere. I rejoice in the promotion and success of others. I know that when I bless others, I am blessing myself, for we are all one. We have one Father or Progenitor—the Life Principle. I am advancing and moving forward along all lines. God is prospering me beyond my fondest dreams."

She reiterated these truths out loud five or six times a day, which helped to prevent her mind from wandering. By repetition, these truths sank into her subconscious mind. I saw a new, radiant young woman a month later. She had become vice president of the organization with a large increase in salary and was engaged to be married to the medical consultant of the company.

Grant to every person in the world the riches of the Infinite and the abundant life, with the understanding that he is ready to receive it when he looks to God as the source and when he loves all other human beings.

He Discovered the Key to the Abundant Life

A Spanish teacher came to see me regarding an emotional problem, which was easily solved. During the interview I discovered that he was very critical of those who had money, lovely homes, Rolls Royces and Cadillacs, yet he also wanted the good things of life and admitted that he needed more money to properly take care of his wife and two children. Nevertheless, he frequently used the term "filthy lucre" and obviously was envious of those who went up the ladder of success in life.

I explained to him that there is nothing good or bad, but thinking makes it so. Money, or paper, is harmless, and our sandwich coins are a combination of certain metals which represent the number and rate of motion of electrons revolving around a nucleus. I pointed out to him that he should look at money in its true significance as a symbol or medium of exchange, which represents man's freedom, harmony, beauty, luxury and refinement. Money has taken many forms down through the ages, and it is simply God's way of maintaining the economic health of the nation.

OPENING THE DOOR OF RICHES TO HIM

The first thing this young teacher learned was that the envy of others was blocking the flow of his good and that the condemning of money causes it to take wings and fly away. Envy of others exalts them but demotes us. God is our source of abundance, and every want can be met instantly and perfectly. To be envious of others is to deny our own good and impoverish ourselves. Envy is inconsistent; it is a waste of energy and is destructive to our prosperity.

DIVINE LOVE IS THE MOTIVE POWER

Love must be expressed. Love is universal goodwill, wherein you wish for all people health, happiness, peace, abundance and all the blessings of Life. Serving people wisely and kindly is really Divine love in action. The Life Principle, or the Cosmic Energizer, must have free expression, and love is the perfect expression of Life. Love is the free and uninhibited expression of Divine Life. Love means peace, wholeness, beauty and perfect joy. Jealousy, envy and condemnation of others indicate a false belief that there is not enough of the riches of the Infinite to go around and the foolish belief that if the other person is a multimillionaire, we shall have to go short of cash. This constricts the expression of Life. Without love we stumble and fall.

BUILDING THE LOVE CONSCIOUSNESS

This young teacher, at my suggestion, began to pray as follows: "I know God is my instant and everlasting supply and support. From this moment forward I sincerely radiate love, peace, joy and goodwill to every person I meet and to all people everywhere. In the college where I work, I claim God's riches and the abundant life for everyone, for I know that Love is the fulfilling of the law of opulence, health, happiness and the abundant life. I give thanks for God's riches which are ever active, ever present, unchanging and eternal."

By affirming these truths, and by their frequent habitation of his mind, a miracle occurred in this teacher's life. All sorts of personal difficulties just seemed to dissolve and vanish. His face had a new glow. He said, "I have felt ten years roll off my shoulders." He has received a promotion and was voted the most popular teacher. His salary was doubled in one month, and there are love, peace and harmony in his home.

Unless we build up within our own mentality a real love consciousness, our various achievements, activities and relationships with others will be somewhat restricted and unsatisfactory. On the other hand, if we become channels of God's love, which is an outreaching of the heart, an emanation of goodwill to all, prosperity and God's abundance along all lines will be yours.

—I am come that they might have life, and that they might have it more abundantly (John 10:10).

ABUNDANCE IS AN IDEA OR THOUGHT-IMAGE IN YOUR MIND

In the charming and beautiful city of Zagreb, Yugoslavia, which I visited in the month of October, not long ago, at the Esplanade Hotel, I met one of the businessmen of the city, who had lived in England for several years. He had read some books published by the late Henry Hamblin, editor of *Science of Thought Review*, from which he gleaned that wealth was an idea in the mind, a mental attitude, a way of thinking. He said he had wanted sufficient money to open up a business in Zagreb, and this is what he did.

He had a silent period a few times a day, and in his mind he was putting money into his business, into his bank, giving money to his sons to buy books and circulating money in different channels, blessing and benefiting others. All this took place in his mind. He knew what he was doing, in that he was gradually building up the mental equivalent of wealth, as one possesses all things by right of consciousness (the union of your conscious and subconscious mind).

He kept this up for about a month, at the end of which time he had a vivid dream in which he found himself at a gaming table in Monte Carlo, Monaco, where he won the equivalent of 100,000 francs, which, when converted to dinars (local currency) was a considerable sum of money. He knew it was an answer to his mental acceptance of wealth. Accordingly, he took a trip to Monaco and experienced objectively exactly what he had experienced subjectively in the dream state. He came back to Zagreb, opened up a shop and found himself able to distribute money just as he had visioned and desired.

Job said:—*In a dream, in a vision of the night, when deep sleep falleth upon men, in slumberings upon the bed; then he openeth the ears of men, and sealeth their instruction* (Job 33:15-16).

Ofttimes in a dream or vision of the night you are instructed exactly what to do to gain your particular goal or objective in life.

SOME COMMENTS ABOUT YUGOSLAVIA

I might add that in Yugoslavia people can own their own business, have bank accounts, etc. It is a socialistic state with a great measure of freedom of religion, travel, speech and expression. Education is free, and a college education is available to everyone. The only thing the student has to buy are the necessary books. The businessmen with whom I talked, as well as our special guide, pointed out that they have an incentive system whereby the man or woman is paid for the quality and type of work he does.

The people are on a capitalistic incentive program instead of the communistic plan. Medical service is free, but all workers pay a small percentage of their salaries under a National Insurance Program. Every family has at least one car. The average salary is from $150 to $200 a month; rent for a good apartment costs about $40 a month. Husbands and wives work and in that way have money for luxuries and trips.

It is a vastly different system than that of Russia or

Rumania. The food and the hotels are excellent, and so is the service. The people are very friendly toward Americans. One guide told me that before they instituted the incentive system, service in the hotels and elsewhere was simply deplorable and disastrous. They do not have the system of collectivism such as is practiced in Russia, Rumania and other eastern countries.

THE LAW OF ABUNDANCE FOR HUSBANDS AND WIVES

It is important for the husband and wife to unite their ideals, motives and activities in order to demonstrate God's riches along all lines. When the two agree that God is the endless source of all good, they will prosper. Agreement means harmony and being harmonious together. They are one with the Cosmic Energizer, which is absolute harmony and the source of all blessings.

A wife who claims that her husband is inspired from On High and that he is God's man and Divinely guided in all ways is one of the greatest motive powers for the demonstration of wealth for her husband. She, too, will prosper because she is thinking of abundance. Since her thought is creative, she is also blessing herself. When you pray for another, you are also praying for yourself.

When a husband and wife disagree and quarrel, there is a scattering of forces, accompanied by loss. This is why so many married couples have financial difficulties. The spiritual minded person never retrogrades. The journey is onward, upward and Godward, for there is no end to the glory which is man.

ANOTHER SECRET TO LIFETIME ABUNDANCE

Practice the law of silence: "Tell no man." This means that when you have a certain plan, goal or objective in life, don't discuss it with anyone except when it is absolutely necessary to do so, as, for example, someone who is directly involved in the plan, invention or enterprise. You can share it with a spiritual advisor, who is there to aid you with scientific prayer. To talk with your friends and relatives is unwise; ofttimes they will ridicule your ideas or throw cold water on your hopes and aspirations.

The less you talk about your ideal, the better. Keep on nourishing your goal with faith and confidence, and when you have established the mental equivalent, your answer will burst forth like a flower in full bloom.

THE DIVINE PLAN FOR LIFETIME ABUNDANCE

Love of God, which means giving all honor, allegiance, loyalty and devotion to the Cosmic Energizer within you, recognizing It as supreme and omnipotent and the endless source of supply, is a type of love which consists of a healthy, reverent, wholesome respect for the Divinity within. Your Higher Self will cause you automatically to love others, and love is the fulfillment of everything. The more love and goodwill you exude, the greater is your share of God's abundance. Your capital consists of the infinite ideas that are in Divine Mind, and God's ideas unfold within you.

Man, knowing his relation to the Cosmic Energizer, becomes a channel depending less and less on outer media and more and more on the Source. We can turn to the Inexhaustible Fountain within, for *God is able to make all grace abound toward you; that ye, always having all sufficiency in all things, may abound to every good work* (II Corinthians 9:8).

POINTS TO REMEMBER

1. Abundance means wave upon wave of prosperity, vitality, happiness, peace, joy and all the blessings and comforts of life. God, the Cosmic Energizer, is the Source of all our supply, meeting all our needs at all times everywhere. Many people are kept in want because they believe it is wrong to pray for wealth. This attitude is rank superstition. God gave us richly all things to enjoy.—*I am come that they might have life, and that they might have it more abundantly* (John 10:10).

2. There is only One Source and One Power. If there were two powers, there would be no order, design or harmony in the world. One would cancel out the other. Infinity is one. Mathematically, scientifically and spiritually, there can be only One Power. Infinity cannot be divided or multiplied. It is impossible to have two Infinities. Those who hesitate to claim prosperity and the good things of life deprive themselves needlessly of these visible blessings.

3. This is a mental and spiritual universe, Spirit (God), and matter are one. These are the two ends of the stick, subjective and objective, visible and invisible. Spirit and matter. Energy and matter. Science uses the word *Energy* instead of *Spirit*, but both are synonymous. Spirit (Energy) and

matter are interconvertible and interchangeable. Spirit and matter are different degrees of the same thing.

4. A talented young lady, attractive and well educated, had received no promotion in six years, yet other girls with far less ability were promoted. The reason was that she looked down on others, felt that they were inferior, and was full of criticism of her associates, saying, "They bore me to tears." We become what we condemn. She learned that the reason she did not prosper and get promoted was due to the fact that her criticism and condemnation of others amounted to self-criticism and self-condemnation, which are destructive mental poisons. She realized that her thought is creative and that what she thinks about others, she creates in her own experience, as there is but one mind. She reversed her attitude and began to exude vibrancy, love and goodwill to all. She made a habit of this through constant repetition. Furthermore, she began to realize that she was a daughter of the Infinite and began to systematically exalt God in the midst of her. This woman's life was transformed within a month. She was made vice president of the organization with a great increase in salary and prestige.

5. A teacher was criticizing those who had wealth, yet at the same time he personally wanted more money and the comforts of life for himself and family. He called money "filthy lucre" and was envious of those who went up the ladder of success in life. Envy and criticism of money were his stumbling blocks to the life more abundant. He learned that envy blocks the flow of his good

and impoverishes himself; he also began to perceive there is nothing evil about money or anything else in the universe. Evil is in man's thought, or motivation. He reversed his attitude and began to wish for all his associates health, happiness, abundance and all the blessings of life. He discovered that love, which is the mood of goodwill to all, is the fulfilling of the law of abundance and security. He began to affirm boldly, feelingly and knowingly that God (the Cosmic Energizer) is the source of his supply and that all his needs are met instantaneously. He also began to claim for everyone he met during the day, "God loves you and prospers you." Every night he gave thanks for God's riches—spiritual, mental and material. His whole personality was transformed and his salary was doubled within one month. He found the peace that passeth understanding.

6. Unless we build up within our mentality a love consciousness, our business, profession, activities and relationship with others will be somewhat restricted and unsatisfactory.

7. When we become a channel for God's love and pour out an emanation of goodwill to all, realizing that God's riches are flowing through everyone we meet, then will we discover that we will prosper beyond our fondest dreams.

8. Wealth is an idea in the mind. A man who wanted sufficient money to open a business of his own began to sit quietly and imagine that he was investing money in his business. In his imagination he was giving money to his sons to buy books and money to his wife to buy a new car. He was also circulating money wisely in different channels, blessing and benefiting others. He acted mentally

the same way he would act objectively if he had the money. His subconscious responded in a dream, showing him how much he would win at Monte Carlo gaming tables. So he went to Monte Carlo and experienced objectively what he had visioned subjectively. The ways of your subconscious are past finding out. He built the consciousness of wealth, thought by thought, picture by picture, mood by mood, until finally it passed from thought and mental image to the joy of the answered prayer. What is impressed in the subconscious is always expressed on the screen of space.

9. In Yugoslavia, the government has established an incentive system whereby a man or woman is paid for the quality and type of work he does. The people are on a capitalistic incentive program instead of the collectivist, or communistic, plan. Prior to that, service in hotels, stores and restaurants was deplorable and shocking. Man is an individual and wants to express himself at the highest level. He wants to be appreciated and recognized. He wants self-esteem. He wants to create, accomplish and fulfill himself. A business or enterprise which has for its aim private gain or personal promotion is no longer looked down upon. One of the guides we had said that there was a time when success, wealth and achievement were downgraded and that mediocrity was exalted. This is no longer true. The tendency now is to exalt and encourage the dynamic and talented dancer, musician, etc., to move forward to new glory and accomplishment.

10. It is important for husbands and wives to unite their ideals, motives and activities in order to demonstrate God's

abundance along all lines. There must be harmony between husband and wife; being harmonious, they are one with and in tune with the Cosmic Energizer, which is absolute harmony and the Source of all blessings. A wife who inspires her husband and claims that God is guiding him, directing him and prospering him will discover that their marriage will grow more blessed through the years, and they will also prosper beyond their fondest dreams.

11. It is unwise to discuss your plans, ideals, goals and aspirations with others unless it is a spiritual counselor who prays with you and rejoices in your success. Your so-called best friend sometimes will throw cold water on the desire of your heart. This is somewhat like plucking the flower before it blooms.

12. Love is the fulfilling of the law of health, wealth, success and constant supply. Love of God means to have a healthy, reverent, wholesome respect for the Divinity within yourself; and then you will automatically respect and honor the Divinity in others. Realize that God is your instant and everlasting supply at all times and radiate love, peace, joy and goodwill to all people. Toward every person you meet, affirm silently: "God's riches are flowing through you and you are getting richer day by day." As you do this, you will find a constant flow of spiritual, mental and material riches flowing ceaselessly, tirelessly and endlessly to you.

—*God is able to make all grace abound toward you; that ye, always having all sufficiency in all things, may abound to every good work* (II Corinthians 9:8).

17

The Cosmic Energizer and Psychic Phenomena

MAN MUST BECOME aware of the tremendous psychic powers within him. It is wonderful to explore the vast reaches of space, but we must also explore the limitless dimensions of our own mind. Actually, man is in the presence of Infinity, and although our astronauts may visit Mars, Venus and other planets in our time, all this wonderful space travel fades in comparison to the wonders, glories and powers within man's own Deeper Mind.

THE COSMIC ENERGIZER GIVES AN AMAZING ANSWER

Recently I spoke before a private club in Reno, Nevada, and following the address a woman consulted me regarding a large sum of money which her husband had won at the gaming tables. She said he had told her that he had won about $150,000 in three or four days and that he was putting it in the safe in their home, to which she had a key. She thought no more about it, and shortly afterward he passed on into the next dimension in his sleep. When she opened the safe, the money wasn't there. She searched everywhere to no avail.

I suggested that we get very quiet, immobilize our attention and think of the Infinite Intelligence within us, which knows all and sees all. We also included her husband in our meditation, realizing and knowing that he was alive with the Life of God and that he was illumined and inspired, his journey being ever onward, upward and Godward. Silently we claimed that the Infinite Intelligence of the Cosmic Energizer would reveal the whereabouts of the money, which she needed.

We remained quiet and receptive for about five minutes, when Mrs. K. said, "Yes, I hear you. I understand. I love you." Mrs. K. said that in the silence she had heard her husband's voice clearly and distinctly, and that it had the same tonal qualities and accent as on this plane. He told her the exact spot in the garage where the money was located and where the key to the box was to be found. Then he added, "I want you to know I am your husband. Remember, we were at a cocktail party the other night at the Palace and you knocked over the cocktail glass and everybody laughed. Also, you lost $15 in the slot machine." Mrs. K. definitely felt that it was her husband, and that night she and her brother went to the garage, removed some boards and found a steel box secreted in a corner. When opened, it contained $160,000 in one hundred dollar bills.

Mrs. K., without any doubt or reservation, affirmed that the message was from her husband. I definitely believe also that in this instance it was her deceased husband who communicated with her. Undoubtedly he had an intense desire to let her know where the money was. It was not a case of telepathic communication between us, as neither of us knew where the money was hidden.

She received an evidential message, and the trivial incident of spilling the cocktail tended to confirm the message as authentic. Consider all the incidents, experiences and material stored in the subconscious mind. Then, when you hear an inner voice with your inner ears giving you a trivial message which establishes without possibility of error that the message originates with a loved one in the next dimension, this is a highly evidential message that your friend is very much alive and in a world of activity and growth.

THE COSMIC ENERGIZER AND YOUR TWO BODIES

Recently on a trip to Yugoslavia, I chatted with a U.S. Naval Officer who had retired in Dubrovnik where he had been born. He writes stories now about life on the sea and of his experiences there. His writing is very popular with children. In our discussion about the wonders of the mind, he thought it to be an extraordinary coincidence that he should meet the author of *Psychic Perception: The Magic of Extrasensory Power*,* a book which had been sent to him by his sister, who lives in San Francisco. He added that his sister knows of his interest in psychic phenomena of all kinds.

He pointed out that while he had had many extraordinary psychic experiences, the most outstanding took place during the Second World War when his ship was attacked by the

---

Psychic Perception: The Magic of Extrasensory Power by Joseph Murphy, Parker Publishing Co., Inc., West Nyack, N.Y., 1971.

Japanese. He and many others had been severely wounded, and before he passed into the unconscious state, he had said, "Lord, save my buddies. Save all of us." Then he said he found himself on board another cruiser in the captain's cabin, where he wrote down the latitude and longitude of his ship and his name and rank with instructions to proceed to rescue the wounded and save the crew. The next thing he knew, he was on board a destroyer, where he was resuscitated. He received brandy and his wounds were dressed. One of the officers asked him to sign his name and compared it with the signature and instructions in the captain's cabin, and it was identical.

THIS WAS A PROJECTION OF HIS FOURTH-DIMENSIONAL BODY

The projection of the astral body, subtle body or fourth-dimensional body, all of which mean the same thing, has been observed and practiced down through the ages. This Naval Officer had an intense desire that he and all his comrades be saved, and his last waking concept was etched in his subconscious mind. The wisdom of his deeper mind knew where the closest ship was located and immediately projected him, clothed in his astral body, which can go through closed doors and collapse time, space and matter, and then instructed him what to do; namely, he was to enter into the captain's quarters and write instructions giving all necessary details, together with his name, rank and location of his ship.

The Bible says,—*In a dream, in a vision of the night, when deep sleep falleth upon men, in slumberings upon the bed; then he openeth the ears of men, and sealeth their instruction* (Job 33:15-16). As you go off to the deep of sleep with a deep conviction that your prayer or desire will be answered, you impregnate your subconscious and receive instructions from the infinite intelligence within, which knows all and sees all.

HE COULD BE SEEN IN TWO PLACES AT THE SAME TIME

Dr. Phineas Parkhurst Quimby of Portland, Maine, who began the practice of mental and spiritual healing in 1847, was America's foremost spiritual healer. He said, "When you think a person is dead, he is dead to you, but to himself there is no change. He retains all the senses of the natural man, as though no change to the world had taken place" (Quimby Manuscripts, page 172).

Quimby could condense his identity and appear to sick people at a distance. He ministered to them, touching them so they could actually feel the sensation. He would put his hand at their head at a long distance; that is, during absent treatment. This was solely to engage the patient's attention and arouse faith. It was a measure of securing the confidence of the patient, at a time when he was starting a new practice and stood alone in it.

In one instance he promised to pray for a woman in New Hampshire and decided to project himself mentally and spiritually in his subtle, or fourth-dimensional body. The woman had a guest for dinner, and the latter said, "There is a man standing behind you." The hostess said, "That is Dr. Quimby. He is giving me a treatment."

Quimby stated, "I know that I can condense my identity

and appear at a distance." In other words, he could be in two places at the same time. He could be in his office praying for a person one hundred miles away, contemplating the Divine idea of wholeness, beauty and perfection for the sick person, and at the same time be present in the home of that person, touching the person and making his own presence known and seen. Quimby knew and demonstrated that there is a Spiritual Presence and Power within man not bound by body, environment, time or space, which is capable of putting on a spiritual body and appearing anyplace.

A VISIT TO A PSYCHIC IN DUBROVNIK

One evening during a recent visit to Yugoslavia, three of us (an Englishman, a German and myself), accompanied by an interpreter, visited a medium in the outskirts of Dubrovnik, one of the most beautiful cities in that country. We walked up four flights of stairs and entered a rather dimly lighted room where statues of saints and icons adorned the place. At the request of the interpreter or guide who accompanied us, the medium went into a deep, profound trance and began to speak in German.

Our German friend who was present said it was the voice of his father, who narrated various episodes in his son's life and identified himself by discussing the most intimate details of his own life. I do not understand German, but our German friend spoke English fluently; German, his native language; and Russian. The medium told him his sister was very sick with a kidney infection and a doctor present with her (in the next dimension) stated she was not getting the right medicine. He said that she should have a certain dosage of a specific medicine, which would heal her.

The German was flabbergasted, and later on after we left the séance, he phoned home to Hamburg to inquire about his sister. He found that his sister was in the hospital and not getting well. He spoke with the doctor and told him what had happened at the séance. The doctor decided to give the drug and the next day all tests were negative; the acute infection had cleared up miraculously.

In the trance state, she said to me (the interpreter translated), "Your sister is here and will talk to you." Then a clear voice came forth having all the characteristics, inflection and tonal qualities of the voice of my sister. She said, speaking in English all the time, "You will recall, Joe, that you fell into the big pond of water near our home in Derrinard (Ireland) and I pulled you out. You were almost drowned and you told about seeing the whole panorama of your life instantaneously. You were nine years old then. You were also lost in the woods one night and all of us searched for you with lanterns and found you crying near a tree."

These were evidential messages of great significance to me. This, indeed was my sister identifying herself and this was not something picked up telepathically from my subconscious by the medium, as I had completely forgotten the two incidents which had taken place when I was about eight or nine years of age. This sister had been a nun in St. Mary's Convent, Lowestoft, England, for over fifty years. She spoke of her transition and of a wrong diagnosis of her condition prior to her demise. She quoted Latin and French verses and prayers which we had learned together. These were identification messages.

The Englishman from Bishop's Stortford, England, was startled when the interpreter said to him, "The medium says your brother who had been an Air Force Officer during the war wants to talk to you." The voice came clearly with a decided Oxford accent. He said, "Mother is here and also Father." He identified himself by very intimate details and spoke of how his plane had been shot down and how he had been met by his parents and cared for in the next dimension. He stated that he was studying aero-space navigation and that our next visit would be to Mars and Venus. His father and mother, speaking through the medium, asked to be introduced to the other two men present, namely, our German friend and myself.

In science, the most plausible hypothesis is one that provides the simplest explanation. In these three instances all of us were firmly convinced as to the identity of each of the communicators and their statements were verifiable in each instance. Any other theory, such as telepathy, thought transference, etc., seems far-fetched and calls for the most extraordinary powers on the part of the medium and stretches man's credibility beyond the point of no return.

THE MYSTERY OF DEMATERIALIZATION

The medium asked each one of us if we would like something brought into the room from our home. The Englishman said he would like to have his walking stick, which appeared in a few seconds on the table with his initials on it. He was dumbfounded and speechless.

The German suggested that an ashtray be brought from his study. This also appeared in about a minute.

I suggested that she bring a Petersen's Dublin pipe which was in a drawer in my study. This, too, appeared.

These are called apports by many, which means the motion or production of an object by a spiritualistic medium without any apparent physical agency. Frequently it has been found that the medium had skillfully concealed the apports in the room or about her person. This obviously was impossible in our case. In cases where the character of the medium is beyond reproach, the idea has been advanced that the result is due to the activity of the subconscious mind. Other explanations are that the apports are actually conveyed to the seance by spirits, or that they are drawn together by some type of magnetic power.

My explanation is rather simple. Modern science knows today about interconvertibility of matter and energy (Spirit). Matter is energy reduced to the point of visibility; therefore, a medium using the powers of her subconscious mind identified with the walking stick referred to in the home of the Englishman and converts it into energy, for the stick is nothing more than a molecular combination, i.e., a group of electrons revolving around a nucleus; and when the walking stick is reduced to its invisible combination of electrons and protons, it is then precipitated by the subconcscious mind in the presence of the medium, taking its former shape.

Think of a block of ice; yet, it is water and with little effort can be converted to steam, which is invisible, possessing an even higher vibration. Water, ice and steam differ only in their vibratory rate. This invisible steam passed over a cold coil becomes water; refrigerated, it becomes ice again. At higher levels of mind it is possible to dematerialize objects and also to bring about their materialization. The whole world is a universe of densities, frequencies and intensities.

The pipe, ashtray and the walking stick could have been brought into the room by a process known as telekinesis, which is the production of motion in a body without application of physical force. In other words, it is possible to transport an object or body by telekinesis. This is called teleportation.

The following articles are taken verbatim from the newspaper *The National Enquirer*, August 5, 1973, issue:

"Cheat-Proof" Experiments at Stanford Research Institute

A topflight team of scientists thoroughly tested Uri Geller at one of America's leading research institutions. Here are the credentials of the men and the institution:

Stanford Research Institute: Independent nonprofit research organization, founded 1946. Supported by research contracts and grants from U.S. and foreign governmental agencies and industrial organizations. No longer maintains any official relationship with Stanford University. Staff of 1,500 professionals, 1,500 technicians and other nonprofessional personnel. Volume of research: 1972—$70 million, two-thirds of that in government contracts.

Dr. Harold E. Puthoff, 36: MSE in Electrical Engineering, University of Florida, 1960; Ph.D. in electrical engineering, Stanford University, 1967. Expert in quantum physics. Holds patents in the area of lasers and optical devices. Author of widely-used textbook on lasers and 25 papers in professional journals. Joined SRI 1972. Now working in area of lasers, biofeedback and biofield measurements.

Russell Targ, 38: BS in physics, Queens College, New York City, 1954. Two years' graduate work at Columbia University. Specialist in lasers, plasma research and paraphysical phenomena. Published more than 25 technical papers in the fields of laser research, plasma technology and optical communications. Pioneer in laser research. Joined SRI 1972.

Dr. Henry K. Puharich: A.B., M.B., M.D., Northwestern University, Ph.D. in electrical engineering, Stanford University. Holds 52 U.S. and foreign patents in medical electronics field. Former senior research scientist at New York University Medical Center. Was president of Intelectron Corp. Author of many scientific articles and two books, *Sacred Mushroom* and *Beyond Telepathy*.

A young Israeli who can apparently bend metal with his mind has undergone rigidly controlled experiments at a leading research institute—and the top scientists who tested him admit they cannot explain his amazing "powers."

Late in 1972, Uri Geller, 26, took part in a series of "cheat-proof" experiments at Stanford Research Institute (SRI) in California, and scientists reported Geller participated in experiments where the probability that anyone could have done what he did was one in a million, and in another test, one in a trillion.

Geller amazed scientists when he:

* Made a balance placed in a bell jar respond as though a force was applied to it—without touching the balance.

A chart recorder monitoring the balance showed that Geller somehow produced a force ten to a hundred times greater than could be produced by striking the bell jar or the table, or jumping on the floor.

* Correctly identified, eight out of ten times, the numbers shown on a die shaken inside a closed metal box.

Only scientists handled the box, and no one knew what number was on the die until after Geller had made his predictions and the box was opened.

* Made a magnetometer, a sensitive instrument which measures magnetic fields, register simply by passing his empty hands near it.

Geller also:

* Bends metal objects and breaks them in half—without physical force.
* Makes objects disappear completely.
* Stops clock hands without touching them.

"There is no question in my mind that Geller's abilities are genuine," said former Apollo astronaut Dr. Edgar

D. Mitchell, now a supporter of scientific and scholarly research in parapsychology who sponsored part of the SRI research and participated in all the experiments.

"We have thousands of feet of film taken during the experiments. In our minute scrutiny of the film, frame by frame, we didn't see anything that looked like trickery in any way.

"At any time where Geller's hands were out of view of the film or it appeared he could have done something in any way to influence a test, we threw out the results.

"We threw out a lot of things that were probably real events just because we couldn't be absolutely certain of them—but what is left we are completely certain of.

"Geller is different than anyone ever tested before in that he can produce results you can see immediately. We have never before seen such great results on scientific instruments. That is what is startling about Geller—and so important." The SRI experiments were conducted by Russell Targ, a specialist in lasers and plasma research, and Dr. Harold E. Puthoff, a specialist in quantum physics who holds patents in the areas of lasers and optical devices.

"We have observed certain phenomena for which we have no scientific explanation," the researchers said. "Further investigation is clearly warranted."

Dr. Henry K. Puharich, researcher in parapsychology and author of many scientific articles, first persuaded Geller to come to SRI for the experiments.

"I had heard stories about Uri Geller before I met him—stories that he could concentrate on watches

and clocks without touching them and the hands
would move forward or backward. He could concentrate
on metal chains and they would break. The stories were a
little fantastic for a tough researcher like myself, who had
been looking at these phenomena for years," said Dr.
Puharich. "But I was soon satisfied that he was the most
remarkable person I have ever found.

"He can concentrate on thermometers and make the
mercury run up and down at will. He has extraordinary
telepathic abilities.

"But probably the most astounding thing he does is
make things vanish. We have had objects disappear for
days and return intact. It is the most extraordinary kind
of phenomenon that man has been exposed to in recent
times."

Dr. Ted Bastin, a physicist at Cambridge University
in England, said of Geller: "The things I have seen him
do are quite remarkable . . . bending metal objects
without ever actually touching them, and moving objects
across rooms. This is a phenomenon we have stumbled
across that might blow apart the reigning orthodox
scientific views.

"Geller directs his attention to an object or set of
objects," explained Dr. Bastin. "He may put his hands
over the object as if he were blessing it, or he may do it
from a distance. It is all very open. He is genuine."

Before meeting Geller, Dr. Bastin secretly bought a
set of screwdrivers. "I left the screwdrivers in a locked
bag in my bedroom. I asked him to direct his attention

towards this set of tools upstairs. They were found some-
time later at the foot of the stairs. I checked my bag and
it was still locked upstairs and apparently hadn't been
touched. And every one of the screwdriver blades had
been snapped off."

Metallurgists later told Dr. Bastin it would be
impossible to break the screwdrivers with the human
hand, and difficult to do it even with the necessary tools.

Recently, prior to an appearance on the Jack Paar
television show, Geller amazed several of Paar's staff by
first bending, then breaking, a key—without touching it.

"If you fit the two pieces together it didn't fit exactly,"
said Paar's assistant Mitzi Moulds, who held the key
while Geller broke it.

"It was as if matter had somehow been destroyed.
I don't have any explanation for it—I tend to be skeptical
about these things. But if it was a trick, I can't figure out
how he could have done it."

. . . He Reveals How It Feels to Perform Amazing Feats of Mind Over Matter

Uri Geller, the young Israeli whose strange talents puzzle
top scientists, told *The Enquirer* how he feels about his
powers and how he first realized he could do things
other people couldn't.

"I believe these are intelligent powers and they are
somehow directed through me. I am a sort of channel,"
said Geller, 26, who apparently can bend metal objects,

move the hands of clocks and transport things from place to place—all with his mind.

The powers that puzzle scientists also puzzle Geller: "I don't know how I do it," he said. "I don't go into any strange concentrations or meditations. All I do is keep repeating in my mind, 'Bend. Break.' And it happens.

"I know I am real. That is enough for me. And the people around me know I am real. The scientists want to keep investigating me and some admit they have no scientific explanation for what I do."

Geller first discovered his powers at age 7.

"At school, I noticed the hands of my watch would jump to a different hour. It was psychokinesis, the bending or moving of an object. I didn't know what it meant, and I thought other people could do it, too.

"Later I found I could concentrate and receive the other student's answers, compare them and get the right answer. I did this until I was 9, then forgot about it until I was 18 and in the Army. It started again and I began demonstrating little things to friends.

"I would bend metal objects by concentrating on them. The most difficult thing for me to do is to bend an object. It doesn't always work. It is like the powers are living somewhere and don't always act whenever I want them to. If something doesn't bend, I have to strike it very gently. It goes faster that way. And in order to succeed, I must have many people around me.

"I would really like to be the first person validated in a scientific institute," said Geller. "I wasn't sure whether anything would happen under laboratory conditions, but to my surprise I succeeded in nearly everything the scientists wanted me to do.

"I am not a psychic," he said emphatically. "There is nothing mystical about me. I do not make predictions and have never tried healing.

"Shortly after I met Dr. Puharich, we were in the Sinai Desert and he mentioned he was sorry he hadn't brought the case for his movie camera from New York.

"I just heard that and didn't think any more about it.

"But the next morning when I woke up, there in front of my bed was the case Dr. Puharich had left in New York.

"To me that is the most amazing thing that has happened, although things happen to me all the time."

In an article in *Psychic Magazine*, May/June 1973 issue, Dr. Puharich, a distinguished scientist, reported that out of 20 attempts to dematerialize metal objects, Geller was 75 percent successful. Out of 20 attempts to rematerialize those same objects, he was 60 percent successful.

In December 1971, Dr. Puharich was in the Sinai Desert with Geller and was complaining that sand was getting into his movie camera. Puharich had left the camera case behind at his home in Ossining, New York. The next morning at 5:30 he got a call from Geller, who said that there was a camera case in his room. "So I rushed over," said Dr. Puharich, "and looked at the damn thing, and it was the camera case which I'd left six thousand miles away in Ossining, New York, locked in an equipment closet, and it was my case with the markings. Furthermore, when I got back to Ossining about eight months later, it was not there, and the one I had was the one that had been there. So that was my first evidence that Uri was capable of transporting physical objects over long distances by unknown means. And subsequently he's done this for me many times."

The preceding articles are very interesting because they demonstrate the powers of the Cosmic Energizer within man, and when utilized and believed in, they work so-called miracles.

Today we speak of the tremendous power of the laser beam, which burns through a granite wall, turning the stone into pure energy and burning a hole large enough to enable a train to go through the tunnel created by this beam of light. The laser beam comes out of the consciousness of man, which is the Cosmic Energizer, the Supreme Spirit, which is omnipotent, omniscient and omnipresent. This Almighty Power has been known to thousands of seers, mystics and illumined men of all ages. The Power is God—the only Presence, Power, Cause and Substance. Everything is made inside and out of It, for there is only One Power.

Anyone can learn to contact this Power and transform his life so that he can perform what the world calls miracles. Within man's own consciousness, or awareness, lies the Cosmic Energizer, stronger, greater and more powerful than all the laser beams and nuclear or atomic power in the world, as all these are offsprings of the One and Only Power. This Power is inexhaustible, limitless, timeless and ageless.

An ancient meditation, lost in the night of time, says:

> Ever the same is my inmost Being, eternal, absolutely one, whole, complete, perfect, indivisible, timeless, shape-

less and ageless, without face, form or figure, the silent presence fixed in the hearts of all men.

POINTS TO REMEMBER

1. Man is becoming aware of the tremendous psychic powers within him. Answers to his most perplexing problems ofttimes come in dreams and visions of the night. Scientists are exploring the inner spaces of the mind and finding an inexhaustible treasure house of spiritual, mental and financial riches.

2. In Reno, Nevada, a woman's husband passed on in his sleep. He was a professional gambler and a few days prior to his demise, he had won about $150,000. He told her that he was putting it in the safe; however, when she opened the safe it was not there. In a meditative state she asked that the infinite intelligence of her subconscious mind reveal the answer to her and guide her to the place where the money was hidden. An inner voice spoke to her, which she recognized as her husband's, giving her all the details and explaining how to remove certain boards in the garage, where she would find the money. She realized that her husband was very much alive, interested in her welfare, and that undoubtedly he wanted to reveal to her where the money was hidden. She recognized his voice and mannerisms, and he identified himself by revealing certain intimacies and episodes in their lives, leaving her with no doubt that it was none other than her husband speaking. Our loved ones are all

around us separated by frequency only. They have fourth-dimensional bodies which are rarefied and attenuated and can be seen clairvoyantly. We do not see gamma rays, beta rays, cosmic rays, radio waves, or electromagnetic waves; yet, these are all around us and interpenetrate us in the same way that the fourth-dimensional universe is all around us and interpenetrates this plane. We go to this dimension every night when men in their ignorance call us dead.

3. A retired Naval Officer in Dubrovnik, Yugoslavia, had an extraordinary psychic experience. He was wounded on board his battleship, and prior to becoming unconscious, he prayed, "Lord, save me and my comrades." He lapsed off into the unconscious state, and the next thing he was aware of was that he found himself on another war vessel in the captain's quarters, where he wrote out the latitude and longitude of his ship and signed his name and rank. In other words, his subconscious mind responded to his prayer and projected his astral body to the nearest ship. All the men were rescued, and when the captain asked each man to write his name, his signature corresponded exactly with the one found in the captain's quarters. This was the way the Cosmic Energizer responded to his prayer.

4. Dr. Phineas Parkhurst Quimby of Portland, Maine, in the year 1847 had the ability to appear in two places at the same time; while praying for sick people at a distance, ofttimes he would appear at their homes and minister to them and could be seen by those present in the home. He knew he was a mental and spiritual being

and that the Divine Presence within him transcended time, space and matter. He said, "I know that I can condense my identity and appear at a distance." In other words, he could be in two places at the same time.

5. While visiting a medium in Dubrovnik, Yugoslavia, this author observed her going into a deep and profound trance, and then, departing from her native tongue, a voice speaking German came through, differing entirely in tone, inflection and quality from that of the medium. The German man present said it was definitely the voice of his father, who told him that his sister was sick and that a doctor who was present with him in the next dimension prescribed a special drug for kidney infection. He followed the instructions, and his sister got well the next day. The next voice was that of one of my sisters, who had been a nun for over 50 years. The voice had all the characteristics, inflections and tonal qualities of her voice, so well known to me. She spoke of intimate details of my life which I had forgotten, all of which were verifiable. She recited prayers in Latin and French, prayers which we had learned together from our father when we were young. These were evidential messages, and it would be a far fetched idea to think they originated in the mind of the medium. The Englishman received a message in a decided Oxford accent from his brother, a former Royal Air Force Officer, who gave details of how his plane had been shot down during World War II. His father and mother, speaking through the medium, asked to be introduced to the other two men; namely, myself and our German companion.

6. In science, the most plausible hypothesis is one that provides the simplest explanation. In these three instances of direct communication with relatives in the next dimension, all of us were convinced as to the authenticity of each of the communicators, and that their statements were verifiable.

7. This medium, in the trance state, was able to bring a Petersen pipe from my office in Beverly Hills and caused it to appear on the table before us. The walking stick of the Englishman appeared with his initials on it. This episode rendered him almost speechless. An ashtray from the office of the German also was projected on the table. These are called apports. At high levels of consciousness, the Cosmic Energizer, which is the Only Presence and Power, can dematerialize an object and cause its molecular combination to condense down and appear at any particular location. Matter and energy are interconvertible and interchangeable. Matter is the lowest degree of Spirit, or Energy; and Energy, or Spirit, is the highest degree of matter. Energy and Spirit are synonymous. Science uses the word Energy for Spirit, God, or the Cosmic Energizer.

8. Think of water, ice and steam. Each one is water, or H_2O, but operating at different frequencies or vibrations. Heat the ice and we have water; boil the water and we have steam, which is invisible, being of a higher molecular vibration. The steam in your iron can be reduced to the point of visibility by passing it over cold coils and we have water, by freezing we have ice. Every metal or substance has its M.P. or melting point, where it can be

rendered invisible. Your body consists of waves of light. Some scientists say your body consists of about an octillion electrons. A man who is highly evolved spiritually and knows his oneness with the Self-Originating Spirit could undoubtedly disappear and reappear at will, i.e., he could dematerialize his body and cause the molecules to coalesce and solidify any place he wished. This is called rematerialization.

9. A young Israeli who can bend metal with his mind has undergone rigidly controlled experiments at Stanford Research Institute. He bends metals and breaks them in half. He stops clocks without touching them. I read also where he dematerialized a watch and reassembled it again. He moves objects with his mind across the room. He appeared on Jack Paar's television show and amazed the staff by first bending and then breaking a key without touching it. In an article in *Psychic Magazine*, May/June 1973 issue, Dr. Puharich, a distinguished scientist, reported that out of 20 attempts to dematerialize metal objects, Geller was 75 percent successful. Out of 20 attempts to rematerialize those same objects, he was 60 percent successful. In December 1971, Dr. Puharich was in the Sinai Desert with Geller and was complaining that sand was getting into his movie camera. Puharich had left the camera case behind at his home in Ossining, New York. The next morning at 5:30 he got a call from Geller, who said that there was a camera case in his room. "So I rushed over," said Dr. Puharich, "and looked at the damn thing, and it was the camera case which I'd left 6000 miles away in Ossining, New York, locked in an equipment closet,

and it was my case with the markings. Furthermore, when I got back to Ossining about eight months later, it was not there, and the one I had was the one that had been there. So that was my first evidence that Uri was capable of transporting physical objects over long distances by unknown means. And subsequently he's done this for me many times."

10. The unknown means of which Dr. Puharich speaks is actually known. It is called the Cosmic Energizer—the only Presence, Power, Cause and Substance. This is the Reality of man. It is all powerful, and man in contact with this power and identifying himself with It can materialize and dematerialize metals and objects of any kind. He can walk on the waters, on red hot coals, and can disappear and reappear at will. I am speaking of a man who is highly evolved and who believes that with God all things are possible. The Power that moves the world is in you. "It was never born; It will never die. Water wets it not, fire burns it not, and wind blows it not away" (Hindu Scriptures).

Ever the same is my inmost Being, eternal, absolutely one, whole, complete, perfect, indivisible, timeless, ageless, shapeless, without face, form or figure, the Silent Presence fixed in the hearts of all men.

—AN ANCIENT MEDITATION.

About the Author

A native of Ireland who resettled in America, **Joseph Murphy**, Ph.D., D.D., (1898–1981) was a prolific and widely admired New Thought minister and writer, best known for his metaphysical classic, *The Power of Your Subconscious Mind*, an international bestseller since it first appeared on the self-help scene in 1963. A popular speaker, Murphy lectured on both American coasts and in Europe, Asia, and South Africa. His many books and pamphlets on the auto-suggestive and metaphysical faculties of the human mind have entered multiple editions—some of the most poignant of which appear in this volume. Murphy is considered one of the pioneering voices of affirmative-thinking philosophy.

Printed in the United States
by Baker & Taylor Publisher Services